Access Audit Handbook

This guide has been produced by the Centre for Accessible Environments
in conjunction with RIBA Publishing.

Text by Alison Grant MA Arch RIBA NRAC Consultant
Case studies by Alison Grant, Paul Highman, Brian Towers and Gill Wood
Extract from an audit report by Cassie Herschel-Shorland BA Hons AMA FRSA NRAC Consultant
Published: October 2005

ISBN 1 85946 177 8
Stock Code 55091

Centre for Accessible Environments
70 South Lambeth Road
London SW8 1RL

Tel/textphone: +44 (0)20 7840 0125
Fax: +44 (0)20 7840 5811
Email: info@cae.org.uk
Website: www.cae.org.uk

The Centre for Accessible Environments is a Company Limited by Guarantee
registered in England and Wales No 3112684, Registered Charity No 1050820.

RIBA Publishing
15 Bonhill Street
London EC2P 2EA

Tel: +44 (0)20 7496 8300
Fax: +44 (0)20 7374 8200
Email: sales@ribabooks.com
Website: www.ribabookshops.com

RIBA Publishing is a division of RIBA Enterprises, a Company Limited by Guarantee
registered in England and Wales No 978271.

Designed by Steve Paveley
Typeset by Academic + Technical Typesetting, Bristol
Printed and bound by Latimer Trend, Plymouth

Contents

Introduction

Who should use this handbook?

This handbook is aimed at experienced access professionals, as well as people who are new to access auditing, who may include:

- business owners, managers and other service providers
- architects
- surveyors
- interior designers
- building and facilities managers
- access groups
- access officers
- building control officers
- equal opportunities officers
- customer services managers
- human resources staff
- health and safety officers
- occupational therapists

Access auditing is a complex activity and people new to the field are encouraged to undergo training. This handbook is intended to be used together with the CAE/RIBA Enterprises guide *Designing for Accessibility*.

Access Audits: a planning tool for businesses

The film *Access Audits: a planning tool for businesses* is available on the DVD supplied with this book. CAE gratefully acknowledges the contribution made by Barclays plc for help in funding this film. The film provides a good understanding of what access audits are, their purpose and how to carry one out. In particular, the film:

- outlines service providers' duties under the Disability Discrimination Act 1995 (DDA)
- explains the role of access audits as a key planning tool in relation to the DDA
- illustrates access audits in practice in three different types of business: a garden centre; branches of a large financial service provider; and a small, family-run baker's shop
- shows how access audits are carried out and what they cover
- explains the importance of active dialogue with the client throughout the auditing process
- describes the way the findings of an audit are fed back to the client, both in written reports and face-to-face meetings to explain and discuss key recommendations
- tells you how to find a qualified access auditor or consultant

Access audits

What is an access audit?

Access audits are an evolving concept and are likely to mean different things to different people. In very broad terms, an access audit is an assessment of an aspect of an environment (building or external area) and services in terms of accessibility. An access audit is a measure of how well the environment and method of service delivery meet the needs of existing and potential users, whether they be staff, visitors, volunteers, pupils, patients and students or others. It is also a process through which potential barriers to access may be identified and recorded alongside suggested improvements in a way that enables people responsible for a site, building or service to move on to the next step of planning and implementing change.

Access audits are not a new concept – they have been undertaken by specialist consultants, architects, occupational therapists and disabled people for many years as a means of assessing an existing environment and services, and identifying potential improvements to facilitate access.

An assessment of access provision in either existing buildings or proposed developments has been a core requirement of many funding bodies for several years, notably the Arts Council and other Lottery distributors. Local authorities have also been required to undertake an assessment of features of their building stock in recent years in accordance with 'best value indicators' which establish the degree to which their premises meet the provisions in Approved Document M (AD M).

The increase in prevalence of access audits in recent years is undoubtedly due to the introduction of the Disability Discrimination Act 1995 and the duties placed on employers and service providers to make reasonable adjustments to policies, practices, procedures and premises where any of these creates a potential barrier to disabled people. The role of an access audit in the process of identifying 'reasonable adjustments' is introduced in the Code of Practice to Part 3 of the DDA – this is discussed in more detail below.

Carrying out an access audit comprises a series of tasks which typically commence with briefing/data gathering, followed by a detailed site survey, consultation with building users and the preparation of a written report to record and communicate the outcome of the audit. Guidelines for commissioned audits are set out at the end of this chapter under the heading *Commissioning an access audit*. The more practical elements of the audit, such as the site survey and consultation with building users are discussed in chapter 3 *Audit methodology* and guidelines for recording the audit data and recommendations in chapter 4 *Report writing*.

> The Centre for Accessible Environments defines an access audit as a means of:
>
> - examining the accessibility of services and facilities
> - identifying where physical barriers may compromise access to services by assessing the feature against predetermined criteria
> - measuring the 'usability' of facilities within a building and the services being delivered in it

The basic principle of an access audit is comprehensively to assess the accessibility of an environment, its facilities and any services delivered from it. To do this, the auditor must take into account all existing and prospective building users and consider any potential barriers that may render part of a building or a service inaccessible or difficult to use by any particular group of users.

Depending on the environment, facility or service being audited, consideration should be given to people who are service users, employees, volunteers and students or pupils in an education environment.

Access audits and the Disability Discrimination Act 1995

The Code of Practice for Part 3 of the Disability Discrimination Act 1995 (DDA) establishes the role of an access audit as key to the identification of potential barriers and associated adjustments within the built environment. The Code of Practice states:

> 5.42 Service providers are more likely to be able to comply with their duty to make adjustments in relation to physical features if they arrange for an access audit of their premises to be conducted and draw up an access plan or strategy. Acting on the results of such an evaluation may reduce the likelihood of legal claims against the service provider.
>
> 5.43 In carrying out an audit, it is recommended that service providers seek the views of people with different disabilities, or those representing them, to assist in identifying barriers and developing effective solutions. Service providers can also draw on the extensive experience of local and national disability groups or organisations of disabled people.
>
> Code of Practice *Rights of Access Goods, Facilities, Services and Premises*

Access audits are not only relevant to service providers. Employers have duties under Part 2 of the DDA to make reasonable adjustments to working arrangements and the physical features of a building, where these would otherwise present a barrier to disabled employees. Although the duties under Part 2 of the DDA relate to individual disabled people, as opposed to disabled people in general, it is still advisable for employers to consider the needs of a range of disabled people when planning an office refit, for example, or looking for new premises. Implementing improvements as part of a refurbishment project or alongside planned maintenance work is likely to be more cost effective and less disruptive than undertaking isolated modifications at a later date. The Code of Practice states:

> 2.11 It is good practice for employers to have access audits carried out to identify any improvements which can be made to a building to make it more accessible.
>
> Code of Practice *Employment and Occupation*

Trade organisations and qualification bodies have similar duties to employers under Part 2 of the DDA, which again relate to individual disabled people rather than disabled people in general. The Code of Practice *Trade Organisations and Qualification Bodies* includes an identical clause (2.10) in relation to access audits as in the Code of Practice *Employment and Occupation*.

Access audits are also relevant to schools and providers of post-16 education and related services. Part 4 of the DDA, as amended by the Special Educational Needs and Disability Act 2001 (SENDA), places planning duties on local education authorities in England and Wales and schools to draw up accessibility strategies and plans which include planned physical improvements to buildings to increase access to education and related services. In

Scotland, planning duties are a devolved issue and the responsibility of the Scottish Executive. Providers of post-16 education and related services have a duty to make reasonable adjustments to buildings where the feature would otherwise present a potential barrier to a disabled student or other person. A responsible body's duty to make reasonable adjustments is an anticipatory duty owed to disabled people at large. Responsible bodies have a duty to make reasonable adjustments where a disabled student is placed, or likely to be placed, at a substantial disadvantage in comparison with one who is not disabled. The Code of Practice states:

> 5.6   Responsible bodies should not wait until a disabled person applies to a course, or tries to use a (educational) service before thinking about what reasonable adjustments they could make.
>
> Code of Practice *for providers of Post-16 education and related services.*

What follows an access audit?

An access audit is the first stage in the process of identifying, planning and implementing change. An access audit should not be considered as achieving an end in itself, but rather a means by which people responsible for a physical environment or service can move forward towards the preparation of an access plan or strategy and the effective implementation of adjustments, whether they be operational, management or physical changes.

The Code of Practice *Right of Access Goods, Facilities, Services and Premises* acknowledges that conducting an access audit is part of a process which leads naturally to the development of an access plan or strategy. Most importantly, the Code highlights that **acting** on the outcome of the access audit, plan or strategy will produce results and mitigate the likelihood of claims of alleged discrimination.

There may be instances where subsequent audits are undertaken of the same premises or service, for example as a part of a continual cycle of review. An access audit is, by nature, a record of a building and its functions at one particular moment in time – it records the features and arrangements in place when the audit was undertaken. Following the audit, adjustments should be put into place which result in the removal of barriers and an improvement in the way services are delivered. Implementation of changes will clearly mark an improvement in accessibility, but should not be regarded as a fait accompli. The Code of Practice encourages service providers to regularly review the way in which services are provided, not simply to consider the issue as a one-off exercise. One way of achieving this is to undertake periodic audits or to review and update an audit previously undertaken. Undertaking a subsequent audit may be

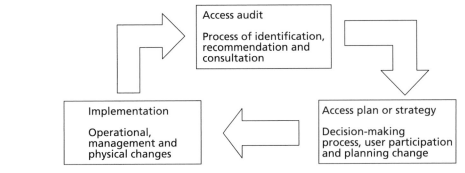

Access audits – a continual process of review

appropriate if the building has been refurbished or if the nature of the client or service provider's business has changed. Undertaking a subsequent audit may provide the best opportunity to update recommendations in line with developing legislation and best practice design guidance.

The case studies in chapter 5 illustrate how the service providers and employers have moved forwards from the initial access audit to plan and implement a range of improvements including physical adjustments, operational changes and staff training.

Commissioning an access audit

Where an access audit is to be undertaken by a person (or persons) outside the client organisation, the fees, timescale, terms of engagement and scope of works should be clarified at an early stage and clearly set out to record the agreement between the client and auditor. The items in the inset box provide a checklist for both clients and auditors.

Commissioning an access audit – issues for the client and auditor to consider:

Terms and conditions of appointment – For the benefit and protection of both client and auditor, the terms and conditions of appointment should be confirmed prior to the commencement of any commission. Terms and conditions should include the client's and auditor's duties under the agreement, payment mechanisms, any requirement for the auditor to carry professional indemnity or other insurance cover, an understanding relating to confidentiality and copyright, any particular requirements relating to communication methods and a mechanism by which the agreement can be terminated and suspended. The AMS (Access Management Services) Supplement to the RIBA Form of Appointment is a suitable model to use. The National Register of Access Consultants (NRAC) has produced model *Terms and conditions for the engagement of an access consultant or auditor*, which is available to download from the NRAC website and can be used for the appointment of auditors and consultants who are or are not NRAC members.

Professional fees – Fees and any relevant expenses should be clearly established and agreed in writing before any work is undertaken by the auditor. Fees will relate to the project scope of works either provided by the client or agreed during discussions between the client and auditor.

Scope of works/project brief – The scope of works should establish which sites/buildings and which parts of a site, building or service are to be included in an audit. This may be particularly relevant where, for example, a client requires only the public facilities in a building to be audited and not the staff-only areas. The project brief should stipulate particular requirements in terms of the audit output, for example the type of report and any requirement for information such as priority ratings, categories and cost bands.

Audit methodology

The site survey

As with any survey, a planned and methodical approach is best. An audit survey, which, by its nature, is an assessment of the accessibility of an environment and its services, is best undertaken in a logical, sequential way. The audit survey follows the 'journey sequence' of arrival, entrance, circulation, facilities and exit. By replicating the sequence in which most building users arrive at and use a building, the auditor can consider the suitability of the environment, its features and any potential physical or operational barriers.

Clearly, larger and more complex buildings will have more than a single journey sequence. Some buildings may have multiple entrance and exit routes, separate areas providing distinct services and defined areas for public or staff-only access. The audit survey should be thorough and fully consider each area of the building, or each distinct area of service.

Depending on the nature of the client business or type of environment, an auditor may be required to be accompanied during the audit survey. Where this is the case, it is useful to know in advance so that arrangements can be made and sufficient time allowed to undertake the survey. Security clearance may also be required and normally has to be arranged in advance of any visit.

It is preferable for a building to be audited when in use as this gives the best picture of how people actually access services and use the facilities. Auditing a building in use may also highlight where there is simply insufficient space for the number of people expected to use the facilities at any one time, a situation which could itself create a potential barrier to access. Auditing a building when it is empty or closed to the public may make the audit survey an easier task, but does not provide an overall view of how the building is used. If the main audit survey has, for practical or operational reasons, to be undertaken when the building is closed, a subsequent visit during normal operation is clearly beneficial.

Where rooms or areas of a site or building are inaccessible because they are locked, in use or because access has specifically been denied, these should be recorded in the audit survey. Clearly, where this is the case, the auditor is unable to assess or record any aspect of accessibility. To protect the auditor from future liabilities should there indeed be an issue with the area, a note should be made that the area was excluded from the survey and the reason for this.

If plans of the building are available, these can be a great help to the auditor, particularly if the building is large or complex. Studying the plans in advance of the audit survey can help the auditor to plan a route or strategy for the survey which will ensure that no areas are missed.

Having said this, where the site or building being audited is one which members of the public visit on a one-off or infrequent basis, it can be beneficial for the auditor to arrive 'cold', without any prior knowledge of where facilities are located or how the service operates. This will place the auditor in a similar position to a member of the public and provide first-hand experience of accessibility in terms of identifying the facility or service.

Where the auditor knows the site or building well it can be difficult to judge how members of the public, perhaps visiting for the first time, perceive the building and its services. Features can be easily overlooked, particularly in environments which are very familiar, and, in such instances, potential barriers could be missed. It is essential in these circumstances for the auditor to consider the facilities from a fresh point of view and to bear in mind how first-time visitors or service users may perceive the environment.

What do you audit?

The elements covered in an access audit depend on the type and nature of the environment and services under consideration. Buildings and sites vary considerably and, although there will be common elements between particular types, no two will be exactly the same. The way services are delivered may also differ between sites which are otherwise physically similar, due to varying policies, management procedures or staff attitude.

Any element covered in an access audit should be considered in the context of the particular environment, site, building or service.

Characteristics of a building, for example whether or not the building is listed, are likely to affect the nature of recommendations in the audit, particularly where physical barriers are identified. Similarly, the nature of a service could affect a judgment made about a building feature. An example of this could be the lighting levels in a nightclub which are typically very low and consequently do not meet best practice guidelines. It would clearly not be appropriate to recommend a substantial change to the lighting levels as to do so would destroy the ambience of the nightclub. Indeed, the Code of Practice for Part 3 of the DDA expressly states that service providers are not required to 'fundamentally alter the nature of the service provided'.

There is no definitive list of physical features, aspects of services or management issues that must be covered by an audit, although the items in the inset table provide a guide to the categories which may be appropriate across a range of building and service types.

Aspects of an environment and services to be considered in an audit:

Publicity and printed material – Publicity material such as leaflets or pre-arrival maps and guides may be the first point of contact with a service provider, building or site. Clearly, not all building occupiers or service providers will produce such information, but where they do and where it is an integral part of the overall information and wayfinding system, the accessibility of the information should be considered within the audit.

Websites – Online information is becoming more common for building and service users, in addition to the availability of web-based services for particular types of business. The way a website is designed and structured can significantly affect its accessibility. Assessing the accessibility of a website is a specialist area and a detailed assessment of any online information is likely to be impractical for most auditors. Reference could be made in an audit report to current guidelines on web accessibility and highlight the key issues for web designers.

Public transport links – Depending on the nature and location of the site, building or service provision, the availability of suitable public transport links may be relevant. The accessibility of the transport itself, the proximity of the nearest drop-off point and the suitability of the route between the drop-off point and the site are all relevant to the accessibility of a venue being audited.

The accessible bays in this supermarket car park would benefit from additional vertical signage to indicate the bays when bay lettering is obscured by snow or leaves, and a hatched safety zone at the rear of the bays, for boot access and cars with rear hoists

Approach routes, setting-down points and car parking – The route of approach for people arriving independently at a site, whether as a pedestrian or by car, is key to the accessibility of a venue. The identification of a site from the approach roads may be appropriate for some service providers, for example the operators of a tourist attraction.

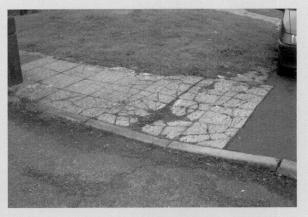

Access routes should be well maintained to ensure that they are safe and easy to use

This poorly designed street environment has resulted in insufficient room between the lamppost and the wall for people to pass

Entrance and reception – The main building entrance should be audited, together with any alternative entrance points in regular use. Most sites or buildings which permit access by members of the public will have some form of reception, security, ticket or information point. Where these are staffed, valuable information about services and any existing barriers to access can be gained from discussions with front-line personnel

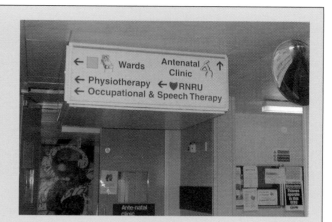

Pictograms are helpful for people with learning difficulties. This sign uses pictograms to reinforce the written word

The shadows cast in this reception area create a confusing environment, which would be difficult for visually impaired people and lipreaders. There is insufficient information and signage, and the lowered section of the reception desk lacks knee space for wheelchair users

Communication systems, signage and wayfinding – These are all essential components which contribute to the accessibility of a site or building. Communication systems may include door entry systems, hearing and speech enhancement systems (for example induction loops, infrared and radio systems), public address systems and visual display units, the availability of communication support services (for example British Sign Language/English interpreters, lipspeakers, speech-to-text display) and audio transcription. The overall system of wayfinding includes the inherent legibility of a site or building, the presence of landmark features to aid orientation, guidance systems and signage.

In this hospital a variety of techniques have been used to convey wayfinding information, including 'talking signs'. These broadcast information as people pass the sign

These signs fail to convey the required information. A new sign, which conforms to best practice standards such as those given the Sign Design Guide, should be installed. Attention should be given to issues such as terminology/language, for example 'accessible entrance', not 'disabled access', capitalisation, font size and colour and tonal contrast

This sign manages to communicate a large amount of information relatively effectively; however, improvements could be made to the lettering by using a sans serif typeface and the careful use of capitalisation

This new and expensive perspex sign is indistinguishable from the surrounding wall. A tatty, temporary sign has been pasted on the wall to communicate the information, because the original design had not been thought through

The accessible WC and the baby-changing facility are both clearly signed, and clearly distinguishable thanks to the clearly defined doors, which contrast in tone and colour with the surrounding wall

Horizontal and vertical circulation – This includes physical features such as doors, corridors, ramps, stairs, lifts and platform lifts. In buildings which are wholly or partly open to members of the public, but where there are potential physical barriers to access within major circulation routes, an audit is likely to include a consideration as to whether services could be relocated as an alternative to making substantial physical modifications. For example, there may be an opportunity to relocate a customer service desk from the second floor of a three-storey building to the ground floor if there is no lift provided.

These steps are potentially dangerous: there are no handrails, corduroy hazard warning surfaces at the top and bottom of the steps, or nosings that are distinguishable in colour and tone

Open risers can be a trip hazard; the stairs do, however, feature a well-designed continuous handrail, which is both warm to touch and contrasts well with the wall

Tapered steps can be a trip hazard for people with mobility impairments and visually impaired people

These highly reflective steps could create a hazard for visually impaired people

This ramp improves access to an outdoor terrace. Upstands and handrails would improve the usability of the ramp. There also needs to be manifestation on the glass surround to the terrace

The entrance to this listed building is compromised by the lack of handrail provision. On flights of steps with a width greater than 1800mm, handrails should be used to divide the flights into channels. Listed buildings often require more creative solutions to access; here the steps could be more clearly defined by careful cleaning of only the risers or the goings

Sanitary provision and activity rooms – The full complement of sanitary facilities should be included in an audit, not just accessible WC provision. All activity rooms, including furniture and equipment, should also be included.

The cistern flush lever is located on the wrong side; furthermore, the position of the radiator and the bin in the side-transfer space would obstruct wheelchair users

Revising the layout of this WC would greatly improve its usability. For example, the flush lever is located on the wrong side, the side-transfer space is inadequate and there should be a drop-down instead of a swing grabrail. In addition, the toilet roll cannot be used single-handedly, the soap dispenser is located on the wrong side of the washbasin, the tap should be located on the left-hand side of the washbasin (closer to the WC) and there is no paper towel dispenser

Lighting and acoustics – The effects of natural and artificial lighting within a site or building can greatly affect accessibility by creating a potential barrier in its own right, for example by presenting a source of glare, or by affecting the perception of other building features, for example poor illumination to a flight of stairs. Lighting issues should be considered as an integral component of the accessibility of physical features such as circulation routes, activity rooms and means of escape, but also in terms of the lighting installation itself, including issues such as luminaire type, position and controls. Similarly, the acoustic environment should be assessed for its impact on the usability of the building and its spaces. Acoustics in a building can be affected by the size, shape and proportions of rooms and by the relative location of quiet and noisy areas as well as by the characteristics of surface finishes.

Internal lighting has not adequately compensated for the glare caused by the external light pouring through the extensive glazed surfaces in this lobby area

Audit methodology

Equipment such as hearing enhancement systems may also be considered an integral component of the acoustic environment, or as part of the building's communication systems, as discussed above.

Surface finishes and visual contrast – The characteristics of surface finishes can assist or impede orientation and wayfinding and may significantly affect the ease of passage throughout a building for all users. As noted above, surface finishes can also affect acoustic conditions and may affect the ease with which people are able to communicate and navigate around a building. Effective visual contrast between surfaces, fixtures and fittings is paramount and can greatly assist visually impaired people to differentiate between features. Textured surfaces are useful in providing information for people with little or no sight.

Tactile paving surfaces can be used to convey important information to visually impaired pedestrians, for example warning of a hazard, or directional guidance. Each type of tactile paving should be exclusively reserved for its intended use and consistently installed in accordance with best practice standards. The misuse of tactile paving, in this instance as a design feature, can be dangerous

Inadequately indicated glass panels. Glazing should be clearly defined with manifestation at high and low levels for safety and visibility

Highly polished floor surfaces can create a reflective and visually confusing environment; downlighters further exacerbate the situation. This environment can be anxiety-inducing for visually impaired people and for people with mobility impairments who may be concerned about falling or slipping on the slippery surface

Although the sign indicates an accessible WC, many people would have difficulties locating the facility due to the complete lack of colour and tonal contrast between the door and the wall. Also, shiny surfaces can be visually confusing

Means of escape – The means and route of escape from a site or building in an emergency is equally important as the route of entry and should be fully considered in any audit. Issues to consider include the suitability and operation of alarm systems, the identification and accessibility of exit routes and evacuation procedures. There is likely also to be a link with building management and staff training issues.

Building management – The way a building is managed encompasses a wide range of issues including practical tasks such as general maintenance and the servicing of equipment. It also includes the way in which staff interact with building users, the manner in which services are delivered and the development of policies and staff training.

The over-provision and haphazard use of signage, coupled with the patterned wallpaper, has created a confusing environment

The excessive signage at this counter is not only confusing, but obscures the view of the receptionist

This reception area has a number of access issues: a plant is obstructing the lowered section of the counter at the reception desk; in the waiting area there is no space for a wheelchair user to pull up alongside a seated companion; and there is no mix of seating with and without armrests

Poorly installed and maintained grabrails are dangerous; this drop-down rail would not support the weight of a user

Survey equipment

The audit survey involves a range of recording techniques, including quantitative measurement and observational assessment. On-site measurements of physical features are essential to the audit survey for comparison with current best practice design guidance.

Key equipment for quantitative measurement includes the following:

Measuring tape – A tape is an absolute essential for any audit. A 2-metre tape is often sufficient and a 5-metre tape will certainly suffice for the majority of audits. Electronic tapes are available which display and 'announce' the measurement, which may assist some auditors.

Gradient measure – An instrument for measuring the gradient of a surface, for example a ramp, path or floor surface, is an invaluable time-saving tool. While some gradients can be calculated (by dividing the length of the ramp or surface by the height of the rise), it is not always easy to accurately measure the rise, particularly for internal surfaces. A tool such as a Gradlevel

incorporates a spirit level, an adjustable graduated 'leg' and a table for reading the gradients for each numbered value on the leg.

Taking detailed measurements within an accessible WC

Using a Gradlevel to measure the gradient of a ramp

Door pressure levels can be measured by using a door pressure gauge

Door pressure gauge – A range of instruments is available for measuring door-opening and closing forces, but the quality and consequently the accuracy of the equipment can vary significantly. As door pressure levels need to be verified with a reasonable degree of accuracy (±2 newtons), a good quality gauge is recommended. Plunger-type models enable doors to be pushed as well as pulled open in order to assess the opening force, which is useful for double-swing doors without pull handles.

Light meters – Light meters can be used to measure the level of illumination of, for example, a reception counter, a work surface, corridor or lift interior. However, it should be noted that levels of illumination can be greatly affected by the direction, intensity and nature of natural light sources and weather conditions, which may distort light meter readings. An assessment of lighting in an environment should in any case take into account the quality of light, colour rendering, luminaire position and potential glare, in addition to the level of illuminance. In this case, it is often better to make an observational qualitative assessment of all these issues, rather than to focus on a single quantitative measurement which could vary considerably at different times of the day.

Observational assessment

Many aspects of access auditing relate to features in the built environment which are not measurable using scientific instruments. Clearly, a different approach is required in these circumstances, as the assessment is observational rather than objective.

Camera and video recorder – A stills camera (film or digital) is an incredibly useful tool for the majority of auditors. Photographs not only provide useful illustrations in audit reports, but are also an invaluable reminder of features in the building or environment after completion of the audit survey.

Video recorders are not essential, but can be used to advantage to record information for the auditor to later review, and can be particularly useful in recording the movement of people in an environment. In addition, a video recorder can be used to provide a 'virtual' walk-through audit, complete with running commentary, for a client to view as a form of audit record.

With any type of camera or video recorder, the permission of the client or building owner should be sought before any photographs are taken. This is particularly important in public buildings where security, confidentiality and public protection may otherwise be compromised.

Visual contrast – An adequate degree of visual contrast between adjacent surfaces, or fixtures and fittings and the background they are viewed against, is important to enable

Converting a colour image into grey-scale can make it easier to assess the effectiveness of visual contrast between surfaces and fixtures. This technique is particularly useful where personal views on colour schemes are likely to affect any judgment made

people with a visual impairment to differentiate between surfaces, to locate items such as door handles and to identify potential obstructions. Visual contrast is established by comparing the Light Reflectance Values (LRVs) of different surfaces. The LRV represents how much useful light is reflected from a surface, with higher value LRVs indicating a higher level of reflectance. LRVs can be measured using a spectrophotometer or hand-held colorimeter. Spectrophotometers are more sophisticated, but are laboratory based and clearly not suitable for on-site assessments. Hand-held colorimeters provide a means of assessing LRVs on site but are limited in application, are not suitable for measuring curved surfaces or gloss finishes and are not currently widely available.

Of more relevance to access auditors is an observational assessment of the degree of visual contrast, taking into account the effects of the ambient lighting. As the effectiveness of visual contrast is predominantly affected by the difference in LRV, an effective assessment can be made of the degree of contrast by converting the view into a monochrome image. Practical ways to achieve this are by photocopying a colour photograph to produce a grey-scale image, by taking a black and white photograph or by converting a digital colour photograph into grey-scale. Each of these relatively low-tech methods provides an image of an environment which may be easier to assess for adequate visual contrast than a view of the full-colour original environment. The effects of reflections from strong lighting may also be more apparent in a monochrome image.

AD M includes provisions for visual contrast which it defines as a difference in the LRV between surfaces of greater than 30 points. The 2005 amendments to BS 8300:2001 *Design of buildings and their approaches to meet the needs of disabled people – Code of practice* (BS 8300) acknowledge that the research-based evidence for the 30 point figure is limited and that anecdotal evidence suggests a 20 points difference in LRVs may

still be acceptable. Differences less than about 20 points may not give adequate contrast. It is thought that LRV differences are less important between adjacent larger surfaces such as walls and floors than between smaller objects positioned against a large background, such as a lever handle viewed against a door leaf. Recent research by the Guild of Architectural Ironmongers (GAI), *Technical Update 3*, confirmed this view. This information is also on the Frequently Asked Questions (FAQ) section on the AD M website.

Lighting – Although lighting levels can be measured (see Light meters in previous section), it is important that an holistic assessment of the quality and effects of light in an environment is made, taking into account the overall levels of illumination, the position, direction, intensity and nature of light sources and the influence of natural light.

It is important to identify existing and potential sources of reflection and glare, as these can be a significant source of confusion for visually impaired people. Similarly, where lighting (either natural or artificial) may cause shadows, or strong pools of light and dark, these should be identified as they may conceal a potential obstacle or be perceived as a change in level or direction.

The positioning of key objects, signs or people in relation to light sources (including natural and artificial light) can have a significant impact on the accessibility of an environment. For example, a receptionist could appear as a silhouette if positioned in front of a window, which would make it very difficult for a person who communicates using lip-reading and therefore needs to see the receptionist's face clearly.

Acoustics – A well designed acoustic environment can greatly benefit hearing impaired and visually impaired people as well as providing a pleasant environment for other building users. Hearing impaired people who have some residual hearing find it easier to

The rectangular sign mounted on the column provides useful wayfinding information, but is unreadable for a large part of the day as it is viewed against a source of strong natural light

communicate if background noise levels are kept to a minimum. Visually impaired people may use different sounds to navigate an environment, for example differentiating between the sound of footsteps on different floor surfaces and locating a lift by the sound of the arrival bell.

A number of observations of the environment and its facilities should be made during the audit survey to assess the likely impact of the quality of the acoustic environment. These include the relative location of areas in the building which may be a potential source of noise intrusion. For example, is the reception desk located at a sufficient distance from the external doors to avoid communications being impaired by external traffic noise? The nature and range of surface finishes in an environment provides an indication of the degree of reverberation. An area with all hard surfaces, for example a marble or tiled floor, plastered walls and ceilings and steel or timber furniture is likely to be highly reverberant and susceptible to high noise levels which could be generated by a small number of people in the room. Softer surfaces such as carpets, mineral tile ceilings, heavy curtains and upholstered furniture all help to absorb sound reverberation and are likely to assist in the reduction of background noise,

but may inhibit the identification of sounds that could aid navigation.

Wayfinding – The ease with which people navigate around an environment depends largely on two factors. One is the 'readability' of the environment or building itself, namely how logically the spaces and functions are arranged and the use of landmark features. The other is by following a specific guidance system, for example maps and guides, or a system of signage which has been applied to the environment. Signage could include visual as well as tactile information. Audio information and audio description can also be used as part of a wayfinding system. Often, a combination of these factors is involved, particularly in large or complex environments.

The overall 'readability' of an environment can only be judged by experiencing the building or site first hand and by considering the experience of other building users. It is often easier for an auditor to assess wayfinding characteristics when visiting a building or environment for the first time, as the experience will then be comparable to that of other unfamiliar visitors. Auditors assessing a building they know well will need to take a deliberate step back in order to consider how the environment will be perceived by first-time or unfamiliar visitors.

Maps, guides and signage can all be assessed for their individual accessibility by considering, for example, visual contrast, text size and style, the use of symbols and general legibility. The position of wayfinding information is also critical to its usability, and an assessment should be made of the suitability of the location, height and relationship to other fixtures or elements of the environment. Of equal importance is the relevance and effectiveness of the guidance system in enabling building users to locate key facilities and exit routes.

Olfactory features – Features in an environment which are detectible by a person's sense of smell can contribute to the system of wayfinding in an environment, whether by design or by default. For example, the deliberate use of fragrant planting adjacent to an entrance can help identify the main route into a building. Cooking smells from the kitchen or carvery in a large pub or hotel may help to identify the location of the restaurant seating area – this is more likely to be an unavoidable consequence of the function of a particular area, but nonetheless a potentially valuable one for a person using senses other than vision to navigate around an environment.

Data recording

Various methods of recording survey information are available and dependent on individual preference. These include taking notes, annotating plans, drawing sketches, completing checklists or a blank pre-prepared table, the use of a dictation machine or dictation to a note-taker, or entering data directly into a laptop computer or hand-held device.

Checklists – Pre-prepared checklists are a useful auditing tool and a great asset on site, particularly for less experienced auditors.

Checklists provide a prompt to the types of feature to look for and, if suitably structured, guide the auditor on a logical sequence in relation to the site or building.

The checklists included in the appendix to this publication are suitable for use in a range of public buildings and cover the various elements of a building and its setting. Many of the individual checklists also suit elements of workplace and other environments. Checklists can be printed or photocopied for use on site, making them equally suitable for a large complex building, or multiple buildings on a single site. Individual checklists can be reproduced several times to record multiple elements of a particular feature, where necessary.

Checklists are regarded as an auditing tool and should not be used in isolation as a report format. They are an effective means of gathering information on site, but require interpretation in order to be of benefit to a client. The data gathered in a checklist requires explanation and should be set out alongside recommendations so that the client is armed with sufficient guidance to progress. Audit data can be set out in either narrative or tabular format, as described in chapter 4.

Pre-prepared tables – The use of blank, pre-prepared tables can be used to record site measurements and observations. This method is particularly useful if the audit report is to be set out in tabular format as it is easy for data to be transferred directly to a computer. If the tables are set up and structured in a logical way, this method of data recording can help to ensure that a logical route is followed around the site or building.

Ratings – Ratings tables typically comprise tick boxes relating to a series of questions. The questions generally prompt a yes/no response, but offer minimal scope for recording the context of any particular feature. Ratings reports may incorporate a scoring system which can be useful to some clients for statistical analysis. This type of report is unlikely to provide adequate detailed recommendations to enable clients to fully consider the range of adjustments that need to be made.

Information technology – The use of computers and hand-held devices offer the opportunity to use pre-prepared databases and templates, either prepared in house by the auditor, or purchased as a ready-made auditing software product, many of which are available on the market. Ready-made auditing software typically includes a series of standard questions relating to, for example, features of the building, plus one or more standard responses, including recommendations for improvements. Such systems can be beneficial to the auditor by providing a question or prompt to measure or observe features of a site in a structured order. Inputting data directly into a computer or hand-held device may also save a lot of time which can otherwise be spent transferring handwritten or dictated notes into electronic format. Despite the benefits, a word of caution is required here. Pre-prepared databases pose a number of limitations for the auditor and can significantly restrict the ability to record non-standard issues, multiple recommendations and to describe a feature in context. It may also be difficult to modulate recommendations to suit different clients, for example a recommendation to overcome a change in floor level in a village hall with limited financial resources is likely to differ from recommendations for the same scenario in a large corporation with substantial turnover. If pre-prepared databases or templates are used, great care should be taken to ensure that all issues are considered in the context of the building/service and that the context for any observations and recommendations is fully considered and recorded.

User participation

One of the most effective ways of finding out about an environment or building and its occupants is talking to regular users, including customers, staff, patients, pupils, students, and so forth. For businesses and organisations, this may also include the business or building owner, the property or facilities manager, reception and customer service staff, health and safety representatives, equal opportunities officers and human resources personnel. Where the building being audited is a community-based premises, for example a village hall, the management committee, volunteers and representatives of user groups are likely to be able to contribute invaluable information in relation to the use of the premises and any existing problems that have been encountered. Existing building occupants are often able to report on problems encountered by service users and on any adjustments which can readily be made to ensure services and facilities are accessible.

As well as discussing how the environment is used, building users may be able to report on any existing links with local access groups and local authority access officers. Advice on making improvements to the building or any services delivered from it may have already been given, and this is often worth noting, particularly where the work has already been or is in the process of being implemented. Where adjustments have already been implemented in response to duties under the DDA, these should be noted.

Once an access audit has been undertaken and a client is formulating an access plan or strategy, the continued participation of users is paramount. The auditor may or may not be involved at this post-audit stage, and it may be more typical for the client to facilitate effective consultation and the participation of service users as part of the decision-making process, prior to the implementation of improvements. Any form of user consultation will be most effective if inclusive and it invites the participation of the full range of building or service users.

Depending on the site or building type, it may be appropriate to facilitate formal consultation during the audit process with a local access group or focus group, as well as staff and so on. This is particularly relevant for major public buildings and for projects where an audit is being undertaken as a precursor to a substantial refurbishment or redevelopment programme.

Consultation may be initiated by either the client or the auditor. If a client is, for example, a local authority, it is likely that there are already established links with a local user group which can be developed to engage views on a particular project. Where there are no established links, the client or auditor may be required to initiate contact with an existing user group or invite representatives from local or national organisations to formulate a project-specific focus group. It is important in all cases that the user group includes members with a broad range of experience of disability. User groups need to represent all users, preferably in relation to user category, such as staff, visitors, customers and so on, rather than consist only of disabled people.

Specific terms of reference for consultation are recommended to be established at the outset to ensure that all parties understand the aims and objectives of the process. Suggested items for incorporation into terms of reference are given below.

Terms of reference for user group/focus group consultation

Aims and objectives – It is essential that the aims and objectives of the consultation process are clarified for all parties concerned. These are likely to include the following:

- to include users in the process of redevelopment of an environment/service and to keep local people informed of developments
- to explore views on specific aspects such as physical features, management and operational issues, communications and interpretation
- for the client organisation to increase their awareness and understanding of user needs

and of how the environment/service can be made more accessible and inclusive

Managing expectations – The consultation process will undoubtedly generate a broad range of comments and recommendations for improving the environment or service in question. However, it may not be practical operationally, or financially viable, to act on every point of view or to implement every recommendation, and this should be acknowledged at the outset. In order to successfully manage expectations, it is useful to provide as much background information as possible about the project, including information such as budget, potential sources of external funding, timescales for implementation and other expenditure commitments so that the consultation group are aware of the context for their recommendations.

Level and type of advice – Depending on the nature of the environment/service being audited and the progress of any redevelopment proposals, the level of advice generated or required as part of the consultation process may vary considerably. For example, if the consultation process revolves around the audit of an existing public building where the client wishes to formulate a project brief for substantial redevelopment, it is likely that general rather than specific recommendations for physical modifications will be discussed as part of the consultation process. Specific recommendations in this context, such as installing a lift in a particular location, may stifle creativity in terms of the overall redevelopment. General recommendations, or options for improvement, may be more appropriate in this scenario. In other situations, for example an audit of an existing museum which is planning to improve display and interpretation material, the outcome of the consultation process could be much more specific and include detailed recommendations on the production of printed, tactile, audio and virtual media.

Reporting and recording procedures – Clear lines of communication should be established, alongside responsibilities for recording and disseminating information to all parties. Minutes of meetings and a record of issues discussed during site visits should be distributed to everyone involved in the consultation process. Alternative formats such as large print, Braille and audio cassette should be produced to suit individual need.

Payment of fees and expenses – Travel expenses should be offered to group members for attendance at site visits and meetings. Where the budget allows, a fee for group members' time should also be offered.

Meeting arrangements – The number, frequency, duration and timing of proposed meetings should be clarified and, where possible, agreed to suit the availability and particular requirements of group members. The venue selected for meetings should be accessible and equipment such as induction loops made available, if required.

Site visits – Where the consultation process involves the audit of an existing environment, it is clearly advantageous to arrange a site visit, wherever possible. This should be planned and arrangements made to facilitate access by group members, where required. If a part or whole of the site cannot be accessed by some members, particular features could be illustrated or described in order to facilitate discussion at a meeting held in an alternative accessible location.

Communication support – Arrangements should be made in advance of any meetings or site visits to provide appropriate communication support to meet the needs of individual group members. This may include the provision of British Sign Language (BSL)/English interpreters, Deafblind interpreters and communicator guides, lipspeakers, notetakers or speech-to-text reporters. Equipment such as an induction loop may also be required.

Building management

The way a building or site is managed can have a significant effect on the accessibility of services and facilities. Poor building management can render a potentially physically accessible environment inaccessible and may impact on all building users.

Building management covers a range of practical issues including caretaking, cleaning, equipment servicing, repairs and maintenance as well as customer service and operational issues. It also covers staff disability awareness training and systems and procedures for implementing and monitoring good practice. The nature and extent of the tasks associated with these issues will vary significantly between, for example, a small community hall and a large campus-style hospital, but are equally important to both organisations.

The effectiveness of a building management system can be partly determined by an observation of the building fabric, namely the overall quality of decoration, cleanliness and whether there are any significant repairs outstanding. However, to gain a sufficient understanding of how the building or site is managed, it will be necessary, as part of the audit survey, to communicate with the person or people responsible for this aspect of work. Discussions should be held as part of the audit survey with property managers, caretakers, cleaners or maintenance engineers, wherever possible, to gauge the general approach to building/site management, how quickly repairs are undertaken and whether regular checks are made of particular equipment such as hearing enhancement systems, fire alarms and emergency lighting, platform lifts and so on.

Response procedures to alarms and call bells are considered to be part of the overall building management system and should be discussed with staff and building users. For example, who is responsible for responding to the assistance alarm in the WC and do they

This signboard conveys useful information about the availability of parking, but is unreadable because the planting has not been trimmed

have appropriate training? Is there a procedure for responding promptly to a door bell or 'assistance required' bell so that people are not kept waiting? In some circumstances, it may appropriate as part of an audit survey to activate call bells and alarms without prior warning to witness the response first hand. However, this is not always appropriate and inadvisable in the case of emergency alarms.

It is also important to identify as part of the audit process the range and nature of existing building management solutions which have been implemented to overcome physical barriers to access. This might include, for example, the provision of assistance to use a temporary ramp, prior to the construction of a permanent ramp and steps to an existing building entrance. The provision of assistance in a shop to retrieve goods displayed at high level or in an inaccessible location is another example, and likely to be typical of many retail establishments. There may be instances where a service is offered to members of the public in an alternative way, such as the provision of a telephone ordering and home-delivery service for goods otherwise purchased from a high street shop. Similarly, where a potential physical barrier is identified during the audit process, recommendations should include not only options to remove or physically alter the barrier, but identify where there is also the potential to provide a service in an alternative way or in an alternative location, if this is relevant to the client.

Report writing

A communication tool

Preparing an effective report of an audit is key to communicating the survey findings and recommendations to a client. A written or video report documents the accessibility of the site, building and its services at a particular moment in time, and may constitute supporting evidence in future cases of alleged discrimination.

An audit report may be the only form of communication between an auditor and a client, for example when the client is a large corporate body and the audit has been commissioned by one department, but the report circulated to several affected departments. It is unlikely, in this scenario, that the auditor would have the opportunity to meet and discuss the audit process and outcomes with everybody likely to see the report. Clearly then, it is paramount that the document carries a full explanation of the purpose of the audit and detailed recommendations which enable the client to move towards the preparation of an access action plan and the implementation of access improvements.

Ideally, an audit report will constitute part of the audit feedback process to the client. Wherever possible, direct communication, presentations, a debriefing or action planning meeting will also be held with the client to fully explain the outcomes of the audit and discuss how best the client can move forwards.

In any scenario, the clarity, quality and effectiveness of the written audit report is paramount.

Report style and presentation

The basic characteristics of an effective audit report are a logical and clear structure, well-written, informative and usable content and good presentation.

The method of presentation can have a significant impact on the legibility and usefulness of an audit report. The style and format adopted will depend on the particular requirements of the client, and should be tailored to meet their particular needs – there is no 'one size fits all'.

Audit reports will typically comprise a printed document but may also be transmitted electronically to a client. Electronic copies of the report provide the opportunity for adjustment of the font size and style to suit particular end users and for the document to be read using specialist screen or data-reading software. Reports can also be integrated with existing building management systems and be easily updated when improvements are implemented.

The categories set out in the box overleaf provide a guide to the type and range of information typically included in access audit reports. The list should be tailored to individual audits.

Use of language – The appropriate use of language is important, and an audit report provides the opportunity for the auditor to demonstrate good practice. The social model of disability supports the use of the terms 'disabled person' or 'disabled people', as distinct from 'the disabled' or 'a person or people with disabilities', which are not good practice. The word 'accessible' is regarded as a more inclusive term and preferred to 'disabled' when describing features such as an accessible WC, accessible or designated parking bay, accessible lift, and so on.

Guidelines for audit report structure

Title page – The title page should clearly identify the name of the report, the site or building and/or parts of these subject to audit, the report author and a document date. The name of the client/person who commissioned the audit may also be included.

Contents page – The use of page numbers throughout the document and a contents page make it much easier for the reader to immediately understand the layout of the report and to locate specific information.

Introduction – This section will typically set the context for the commission and may include brief details of the site, building or services being audited.

Client brief/scope of audit – The scope of the audit will reflect the client brief; it will establish which parts of the building and service are to be included in the audit and any exclusions. It may also include specific reasons for carrying out the audit, such as in connection with a funding application. As described in chapter 2 *Commissioning an access audit*, the brief should indicate particular requirements in terms of output, for example the type and format of the report and any requirement for specific information such as priority ratings, categories for recommendations and cost bands.

Audit details – The site and/or building name and address, date of the audit survey and name of the auditor should be clearly recorded.

Description of site/building and functions – It is useful to provide a description of the site and/or building being audited, including information such as ownership, approximate size/area, number of floors, type of construction and age. If the building or any feature is listed, this should be noted, as it is likely to affect the nature of any recommendations. An explanation should be included of how the site or building is used, whether some areas are restricted to staff-only access, and whether access is available to members of the public, as this information is key to the audit process, particularly in the context of various duties under the DDA.

Legislative context – Given that the majority of access audits are commissioned in the context of the DDA, a section setting out the background to the Act and the key duties, as relevant to the site, building or client in question, is particularly important.

Criteria for assessment – The benchmark by which observations and recommendations are made should be clearly set out and is likely to comprise a list of documents including Approved Document Part M, BS 8300:2001, relevant local design guides, other publications and client requirements for inclusive access. An explanation should be included to clarify how these documents relate to the DDA.

Explanation of priorities and categories – Prioritisation of recommendations is particularly valuable for the client, and it is important to explain the basis of prioritisation and categorisation.

Disclaimer – It is advisable to clearly set out the limitations of the audit report. The DDA is not compliance based and not prescriptive in its requirements; therefore, clients should be advised that adherence to the recommendations in the report does not provide immunity from prosecution under the Act. However, disclaimers are of limited practical value and anyone proposing to rely on one should seek legal advice.

Summary (or executive summary) – It is useful, particularly for lengthy reports, to include a summary which highlights the key issues in the audit. The summary can be used to provide a brief overview of the current accessibility of the site/building and to identify significant recommendations.

Main body of audit – This is likely to be the most substantial part of the audit report and will record the details of the audit survey and set out recommendations for potential improvements. The way in which this information is set out is likely to depend on the client's requirements and the size and complexity of the building. Some examples of different report formats are discussed on the pages to follow, including narrative and tabular reports.

Appendices – These can be used to set out supplementary information such as design guidance, general recommendations, photographs (if not included in the main body of the report), site or building plans, a copy of an organisation's access policy or other supporting documents, a list of useful contacts and a bibliography.

Terms to be avoided when making recommendations include any phrase which implies or suggests that a particular feature 'complies' with the DDA. Service providers and employers may indeed comply with their respective duties under the Act, by making reasonable adjustments in relation to services and employment practices. This would be an appropriate use of the term 'comply'. However, the DDA does not include prescriptive guidance on the design or provision of building features and it would be misleading to suggest that the provision of, for example, an accessible WC or a ramp at a specific gradient, would 'comply' with the DDA. The provision of a particular physical feature does not in itself ensure or necessarily demonstrate 'compliance' with the DDA.

The use of clear English throughout the report is paramount as this will greatly improve legibility and clarity for all readers. The use of jargon should be avoided, particularly for non-technical clients.

Report formats

There are many different formats for audit reports and the use of any one particular format will depend on the nature and type of site or building and on the needs of the client. No one type of format will suit all clients or all audits – a format should be developed that communicates the outcome of the audit most effectively to the client.

Two of the more commonly used report formats are described below – these are categorised as narrative and tabular reports.

Narrative reports

Narrative audit reports are characterised by detailed descriptive text. The report style is typically lengthy and includes a clear description of existing features, an explanation as to why particular features may present a potential barrier and detailed recommendations for potential improvements. Narrative reports are an effective way to discuss particular features in the overall context of the building. This style of report is generally more readable than structured tabular reports and may therefore be more suitable for non-technical clients. Such reports are usually more suited to smaller sites or buildings.

Narrative reports also provide a suitable format for walk-and-talk audits where an auditor undertakes a site survey with the client, discusses key issues while on site and

Narrative audit report example

10 Internal stairs

The internal stairs link the upper and lower floors and provide a fire exit route from the first-floor main hall. The stairs are wide (1500mm between walls), and the steps have 300mm tread and 170mm riser dimensions, which are all considered suitable. The stairs are L-shaped in arrangement and comprise two flights of 10 steps, each with a rise of 1700mm, and an intermediate landing 1500mm long. This arrangement meets the provisions of AD M 3.51 which recommends a maximum of 12 risers between landings. There are handrails to both sides, although they are not continuous around the corner of the stair. The handrails are formed from a rectangular section of timber board and are currently painted the same colour as the walls. The step nosings incorporate a broad black and white strip which is viewed against a dark blue vinyl finish to the tread and riser surfaces. This is a potential source of confusion, particularly for a visually impaired person. The artificial lighting arrangement appears to provide a suitable and even level of illumination to the full length of the flight and top and bottom landings.

The overall stair arrangement is considered suitable, although improvements could be made to benefit all building users. Improvements include replacing the handrail with a continuous tubular rail to both sides of the stair – tubular-type rails are much easier to grip than flat boarding. The handrail should also contrast in colour with the wall so that it is easier to distinguish. It is also suggested that the marking of step nosings be replaced to provide a single contrasting band of colour. (AD M p 24) The contrasting marking on the nosing is provided to identify the edge of the step

– if two bands of colour are used, it may not be clear which band marks the change of level.

Summary of recommendations:

- Replace the markings of stair nosings so that a single band of contrasting colour is used to identify the edge of the step.
- Replace the handrail to both sides of the stairs. The handrail should be a tubular type, 40–45mm in diameter, and mounted with a clearance between the wall and handrail of 60–75mm. The handrail should contrast in colour with the wall surface. The handrail should be continuous to the full length of the stairs, including landings, and should project horizontally 300mm beyond the top and bottom step.

prepares a brief written record of the visit, summarising key points.

Tabular reports

Tabular reports, as their name suggests, comprise a series of tables used to set out and structure information. In tabular reports, text and descriptions are generally more succinct compared to narrative reports, but should still be sufficiently detailed to provide usable information for the client.

Tabular reports can be used for any size of building, but are particularly suitable for larger sites or buildings where a narrative report would otherwise be too long and unwieldy. Data can be easily extracted from tabular reports, as long as the information is set out in a logical order and clearly referenced – this may be an advantage if a client is collating information in a particular category, for example surface finishes across a number of different floor levels.

When undertaking the audit survey, pre-prepared tables can be used to record site measurements and observations. This method of data recording can help to ensure a logical route is followed around the site or building, if the tables are set up in a structured way.

Tables can easily be expanded to incorporate particular information required by the client, for example priority ratings, categories and cost bands. Where audit reports are provided in electronic format, clients can import data into their own database and add columns to record progress, cost and any other relevant details.

An example of a tabular audit report is in chapter 6 *Extract from an audit report.*

Establishing the legislative context

Many audits are carried out in response to duties placed on clients by the Disability Discrimination Act 1995 (DDA). It is therefore important to provide clear information about the relevant sections of the DDA and how they might apply to a particular client. For example, if an audit is carried out of a school for its governing body, they will need information on Part 2, Part 3 and Part 4, including information on their planning duty under Part 4 of the DDA; a high street retailer will need information on Part 2 (for staff areas) and Part 3 (for public areas); an organisation with employees, but not providing a service to the general public, will most likely only need information on Part 2. Clients may also need to be aware of any duties they may have in relation to the Disability Discrimination Act 2005.

However, the role of the access auditor or consultant is not that of a legal advisor. There may be situations when it is not clear how the DDA affects the client. In such cases, it is important to recommend that clients seek appropriate legal advice.

It is also important to be clear about the limitations of the guidance contained within the report. An access audit is not a legal requirement, but is recommended in the various Codes of Practice that support the Act.

It should also be made clear, through the use of a disclaimer clause in the report, that acting on the recommendations of the report does not guarantee 'compliance' with the DDA.

The use of timescales and priorities must be appropriate to the circumstances and agreed with the client in advance. If a priority highlights works that are required within a year, the report needs to make it clear why this is so and who has made the decision. The client's duty is to make reasonable adjustments to ensure disabled people are not discriminated against unjustifiably. The reasonable adjustment might be to provide the service by reasonable alternative means, and may require no physical alterations.

It is the client's responsibility to develop an access strategy/plan and to act upon it. The audit report and the recommendations and priorities contained within it will assist this process. The incorrect use of priorities and lack of clarity as to how they are related to the DDA may result in clients carrying out expensive and inappropriate works. Priorities should distinguish where different parts of the DDA apply in relation to the premises and services. A feature identified as a significant barrier may be a high priority if the area is public; however, if the area is restricted to employees and it does not present a barrier to any of them, then making an adjustment would only be required as a matter of good practice.

Criteria for assessment and design guidance

To establish validity for observations and recommendations made in the audit, it is important to set a benchmark by which existing features are assessed. As previously discussed, the DDA provides no specific design or dimensional guidance in relation to physical features. The Act sets out duties for service providers, employers and others to make 'reasonable adjustments', but does not stipulate what the adjustments should be and does not set down any specific design criteria. The Codes of Practice to the Act do, however, make reference to specific sources of design guidance, these being Approved Document M (England and Wales), the Technical Standards (Scotland), Technical Booklet (Northern Ireland) and BS 8300. The Codes of Practice also refer to 'the wealth of published advice on the principles and practice of "inclusive design"'. The sources directly quoted are minimum requirements and it is preferable to meet best practice guidance.

Building regulations

England and Wales – In England and Wales, building design and construction are governed by the Building Regulations. These regulations comprise a series of requirements for specific purposes: health and safety, energy conservation, prevention of contamination of water and the welfare and convenience of persons in or about buildings.

Building Regulations are supported by Approved Documents which give practical guidance with respect to the regulations. While their use is not mandatory – and the requirements of regulations can be met in other ways – Approved Documents are used as a benchmark by building control authorities and approved inspectors. The new Approved Document M (AD M), which

Cover of AD M

came into effect in May 2004, offers technical guidance on providing access to and within buildings. It is informed largely, although not wholly, by the dimensional criteria in the BS 8300.

Scotland – On 1 May 2005 a new building standards system came into force in Scotland. The Building (Scotland) Act 2003 gave Scottish Ministers the power to make building regulations which are administered by the Scottish Building Standards Agency (SBSA), a new executive agency of the Scottish Executive.

The building standards are supported by two new Technical Handbooks: a Domestic Handbook and a Non-domestic Handbook. The Handbooks provide guidance on achieving the standards set in the Building (Scotland) Regulations 2004. Access requirements are integrated into the Technical Handbooks, as they were in the previous Technical Standards.

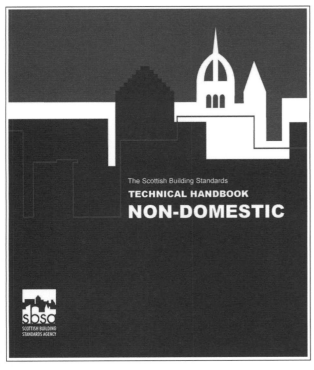

Cover of new Non-domestic Technical Handbook

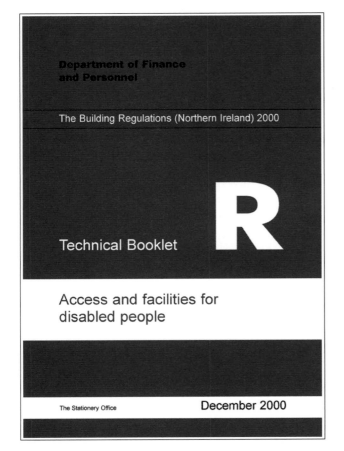

Cover of NI Technical Booklet

Northern Ireland – In Northern Ireland, Part R of the Building Regulations (NI) covers *Access and Facilities for Disabled People*, and is supported by Technical Booklet R:2000.

The provisions in AD M, the Technical Handbooks and Technical Booklets represent minimum standards. It is preferable, in many circumstances, to consider going beyond these standards to meet best practice guidelines.

BS 8300:2001 (Incorporating Amendment No. 1) *Design of Buildings and their approaches to meet the needs of disabled people – Code of practice*

BS 8300 provides comprehensive guidance relating to access to buildings for disabled people. The document provides detailed guidance on good practice for the design of a range of building types, including workplace and public buildings. Although generally applying to new buildings, BS 8300 provides useful guidance and dimensional criteria that can be used to assess the accessibility of existing buildings.

Many of the design recommendations in BS 8300 are based for the first time on ergonomic research commissioned in 1997 and 2001 by the Department of the Environment, Transport and the Regions. The recommendations apply to car-parking provision, setting-down points and garaging, access routes to and around all buildings, and entrances to and interiors of new buildings. BS 8300 includes commentary which provides a context and rationale for the design guidance. Management and maintenance issues are incorporated in recognition that these play an essential part in the delivery of accessible services and facilities to disabled people.

The revised BS 8300, published in June 2005, has aligned the BS with AD M on many issues, including dimensions of handrails, door opening and closing forces and the application of light reflectance values.

Cover of BS 8300:2001

The Office of the Deputy Prime Minister (ODPM), who is responsible for writing the Approved Documents, has published some of these amendments made to BS 8300 on a Frequently Asked Questions (FAQ) page concerning Approved Document M on the Building Regulations section of their website www.opdm.gov.uk. The two documents are thus now usefully aligned and provide non-conflicting advice.

Reference to BS 8300 as part of the audit process is particularly valuable where features of a site or building are not otherwise covered by AD M (England and Wales), the Non-domestic Technical Handbook (Scotland) or Technical Booklet (Northern Ireland). These supporting documents to the relevant building regulations and standards only cover features which can be monitored through the building control process. BS 8300 has a much wider remit and covers features of an environment that are key to accessibility but do not come within the remit of the building control authorities and approved inspectors. A few examples of this include the suitability of floor finishes, the detailed design of signage, the height of shelving and reception counters.

The Appendices include a list of publications, many of which provide design guidance and best practice advice on the provision of accessible facilities and services. Some documents provide general advice which is applicable to a range of public buildings, while others provide specific advice on particular features or building types.

Some larger organisations, notably local authorities, publish in-house design guides to support a practical approach to inclusive design. Many such guides are developed in partnership with local access groups and set a benchmark which often goes beyond the minimum provisions of national guidance such as AD M, the Scottish Technical Manuals and BS 8300. Grant-making bodies sometimes have their own standards and criteria. While such design guides are unlikely to be mandatory, they are produced and published in order to promote best practice in inclusive design in a particular area. Where such guides exist and are relevant, they should form part of the benchmark criteria.

There will be occasions when a particular physical feature is not covered in design guidance and the basis for recommending change is undefined. An example of this might be the provision of baby-changing facilities. Their incorporation into accessible WC facilities is discouraged, but they are not clearly defined in any other context. There is very little design guidance available specifically relating to the design and layout of accessible baby-changing facilities, although their provision should be considered where such facilities are available. Dimensional and other design criteria in this scenario are likely to be derived from an understanding of the spatial requirements, recommended counter heights, reach ranges and visual contrast covered by existing design guidance for other building features and applied to the particular building being audited.

There may also be instances where a feature is provided in a building which does not accord with published design guidance, but has been provided for a specific purpose and should be retained in its existing configuration. An example of this might be an accessible WC facility in a large primary school which achieves the minimum overall room dimensions, but has been equipped with sanitaryware and handrails that do not accord with the layout in AD M. The sanitaryware and handrails have, in fact, in this example, been positioned to meet the specific needs of a disabled pupil and should clearly not be altered as long as they continue to meet the pupil's needs. What the auditor should be considering in this scenario is whether the accessible WC is likely to also meet the needs of other disabled people, whether the provision of a single accessible WC is sufficient for the whole school and whether an additional accessible WC facility, equipped in accordance with the provisions of AD M is required to meet the needs of disabled visitors. Situations such as this require the auditor to keep an open mind and, critically, to enquire about the use of existing facilities from building users. It is rare that any building will follow a precise blueprint and strictly accord with published design guidance – the auditor should make considered judgments in the overall context of the site and/or building and the nature of the service provided.

Making recommendations

In many respects, the recommendations are the most important aspect of an access audit – they provide the client with a clear direction for making decisions and implementing

change. In order to be effective, recommendations must be clearly set out, thoroughly explained and sufficiently detailed to enable the client to make decisions and take action.

It is preferable that recommendations are made on the basis of an inclusive design approach that seeks to ensure that everyone can access and benefit from the full range of opportunities available in society. The ODPM *Good Practice Guide: Planning and Access for Disabled People, 2003* says inclusive design 'aims to remove barriers which create undue effort, separation or special treatment and enables everyone to participate equally in mainstream activities independently with choice and dignity'.

According to the Centre for Accessible Environments, inclusive design:

- places people at the heart of the design process
- acknowledges human diversity and difference
- offers choice where a single design solution cannot accommodate all users
- provides for flexibility in use
- aims to provide buildings and environments that are convenient, equitable and enjoyable to use by everyone, regardless of ability, age and gender

Inclusive design is an evolving field and subject to continual review and, in some cases, structured research. Design guidance considered today as representing best practice may tomorrow be amended, expanded or superseded. In many cases, design guidance will be expanded as further research and experience is gained in a particular subject area. However, there will be instances, particularly where equipment and safety requirements evolve, where facilities previously considered acceptable in certain circumstances are no longer recommended. An example of this is the provision of chair stairlifts in public buildings which were permissible in certain circumstances under the provisions of the 1999 edition of AD M, but are no longer considered suitable. Auditors should keep abreast of all such developments to ensure that advice given in audits is up to date.

The key issue for auditors, and one that is often overlooked, is that there is usually more than one way of overcoming a potential barrier to access. There may indeed be several ways of improving access to or usability of a feature or service, including the implementation of permanent physical modifications, temporary physical adjustments, the provision of equipment, changes in management strategy, or changes to the location or the way a service is delivered. Some solutions can offer immediate improvements to the way services are delivered, others provide short-term solutions and some provide permanent improvements, but may take some time to implement. All of these options are relevant and accord with the list given in the Code of Practice for Part 3 of the DDA:

> 5.31 Where a 'physical feature' makes it impossible or unreasonably difficult for disabled people to make use of any service which is offered to the public, a service provider must take reasonable steps to:
>
> - remove the feature; or
> - alter it so that it no longer has that effect; or
> - provide a reasonable means of avoiding the feature; or
> - provide a reasonable alternative method of making the service available to disabled people.
>
> Code of Practice *Rights of Access Goods, Facilities, Services and Premises*

Although the list of options for overcoming a physical barrier is written 'top down', with what is likely to be the most desirable item (but potentially the most costly) at the top of the list, there is in fact nothing in the Act which stipulates the way in which a service provider

should meet their obligations. The focus of the Act is that services are made accessible – the manner in which this is achieved is for the service provider to consider. Having said this, the Code of Practice encourages an inclusive approach to the provision of services and does in fact suggest that the removal of a feature may represent the best option.

> 5.38 It is in the interests of both service providers and disabled people to overcome physical features that prevent or limit disabled people from using the services that are offered. Although the Act does not place the different options for overcoming a physical feature in any form of hierarchy, it is recognised good practice for a service provider to consider first whether a physical feature which creates a barrier for disabled people can be removed or altered.
>
> 5.39 This is because removing or altering the barriers created by a physical feature is an 'inclusive' approach to adjustments. It makes the services available to everyone in the same way. In contrast, an alternative method of service offers disabled people a different form of service than is provided for non-disabled people.
>
> 5.40 Removing or altering the barriers created by a physical feature will also be preferable to any alternative arrangements from the standpoint of the dignity of disabled people. In addition, it is likely to be in the long-term interests of the service provider, since it will avoid the ongoing costs of providing services by alternative means and may expand the customer base.
>
> 5.41 Therefore, it is recommended that service providers should first consider whether any physical features which

create a barrier for disabled people can be removed or altered. If that is not reasonable, a service provider should then consider providing a reasonable means of avoiding the physical feature. If that is also not reasonable, the service provider should then consider providing a reasonable alternative method of making the service available to disabled people.

Code of Practice *Rights of Access Goods, Facilities, Services and Premises*

An important factor which is likely to influence the range and type of recommendations set out in a report is the timescale for implementation. If the recommendations include the construction of a new ramp and steps to the main entrance of a public building, it is likely to take several months to obtain the necessary planning and building regulations approvals, plus any listed building or landlord consents where relevant. During the process of obtaining consents and at all times up until the ramp and steps are available for use, the service provider still has a duty to make reasonable adjustments to ensure the services in the building are accessible. In the intervening period, this could be achieved in a number of ways, such as providing an alternative accessible entrance, providing a temporary ramp, providing the service in an alternative accessible location or in an alternative way.

This example illustrates that, even where a client does proceed with a permanent physical modification, other solutions for overcoming a physical barrier cannot necessarily be ruled out as they may offer more immediate and short-term alternatives which are key to the availability and accessibility of services.

The factors which influence any decision about what constitutes a 'reasonable adjustment' under Part 3 of the DDA include the effectiveness and practicality of the change, the extent of disruption, the cost of the work and the resources available, the amount of money already spent on adjustments and the availability of financial or other forms of assistance. It is rare for an auditor to have a comprehensive knowledge of how all these issues affect a client, particularly the issue of available resources. As a result, it is clearly inappropriate for an auditor to make finite recommendations which involve significant expenditure, without also offering alternative solutions which are better suited to clients with potentially fewer resources. This is not an opportunity to get away with providing a less expensive solution, it is a thorough explanation of the alternatives available and should provide sufficient information for the client to make an informed decision on how to proceed.

To what level of detail should recommendations be made? This will depend on a range of factors, including the client's information requirements and particular details of the commission. It is also likely to relate to the client's degree of awareness of access issues and their understanding of relevant legislation. Where recommendations relate to physical modifications, a client's technical knowledge and understanding of the building development processes may influence the degree to which design and dimensional guidance are set out.

For example, the management committee of a community building comprises members representing each of the user groups, none of whom has technical or construction knowledge. Some members have experience of particular disabilities, but none has a comprehensive understanding of access or legislative issues. For an audit of the site, building and facilities for this community building to be effective and enable the management committee to make informed decisions, the recommendations will need to clearly explain the options available, why they represent an improvement in accessibility and, where adjustments relate to physical features, give sufficient design and dimensional guidance to fully explain the nature of work. In this scenario, a simple statement such as 'redecorate internal surfaces' is unlikely to be sufficient. The audit should explain the benefits of visual contrast between surfaces and fixtures to people with a visual impairment so that the client is aware of the reason behind the recommendation. It should be clear which elements of the interior should be redecorated to maximise the benefits of visual contrast. Wherever possible, guidance could also be given on sources of further information, as long as these are readily available to the client.

Undertaking an audit of, for example, a local authority premises, commissioned by the estates department in order to identify potential physical improvements prior to a major refurbishment project, is likely to involve a different emphasis when drafting recommendations. As the recipient of the audit report is undoubtedly from a technical background, detailed reproduction of design and dimensional criteria may not always be necessary. Of more relevance is a discussion of any options available for improving access and a consideration of how physical aspects of the building interrelate with operational and management issues.

However recommendations are drafted, it is essential that they are sufficiently detailed and explained to enable the client to make informed decisions and to move on to the next stage in the process of improvements.

Priorities and categories

It is good practice to prioritise and categorise recommendations. From a client's point of view, guidance on the degree of priority for addressing a particular barrier to access is clearly valuable, but from the auditor's point of view, much harder to establish.

Priority ratings and categories, where used, should be established in consultation with the client and clearly defined in the audit report.

Priority ratings

By definition, priorities have an inherent sense of importance and a degree of urgency. Priorities should be attributed to recommendations in the context of the client's circumstances.

A word of caution is required here. Priority ratings are often confused with categories which can be misleading to the client. For example, priority ratings defined as 'adjustments that can be made immediately', 'work to be undertaken in the next 12 months' and 'major modifications requiring longer term planning' do not necessarily reflect the importance of a particular recommendation. The installation of a passenger lift in an existing multi-storey building to which members of the public have access on all floor levels, but which currently has no alternative means of vertical circulation other than the stairs, is likely to be a high priority for the client. However, in the example above, the recommendation to install a lift is likely to fall into the third definition, that is, 'major modifications requiring longer term planning'. Being third on the list, the priority rating has, by implication, a reduced sense of importance which is clearly inappropriate for this item of work. The definitions in this example would, in fact, be more appropriately termed categories, as they are classifying work into divisions which simply record how quickly the work could be achieved.

Priority definitions should be established which enable any recommendation to be attributed the appropriate degree of importance, irrespective of the size or nature of the work.

Priority ratings

Example 1

A   Items which are likely to significantly improve the accessibility of services and facilities and are strongly recommended for immediate consideration. Also, any item constituting a risk to the health and safety of building users.

B   Additional recommended action to meet best practice guidelines which are likely to improve accessibility for all building users.

Example 2

A   **Essential** – indicates that the work recommended is essential to provide access which would otherwise be impossible or unsafe.

B   **Desirable** – indicates that the work recommended is necessary to ensure independent access for some disabled people.

C   **Best practice** – indicates that the work is required to improve accessibility for all, and ensure that best practice standards are achieved.

Categories

Example 1

B	Building modification
I	Interpretation
M	Management
H&S	Health and Safety
T	Staff training

Example 2

M	Management
B	Building element (structure and building services)
E	Estates (long-term development to be considered)
T	Training (staff)
O	Other (for example Highways)

Example 3

M	Work could be carried out as part of an ongoing maintenance programme
R	Indicates that work may be necessary to suit a known individual member of staff
O	Indicates that other organisations or authorities may need to provide specialist input or sanction improvements

Categories

Categories represent a system of classification which enables audit recommendations to be attributed to various divisions. The divisions may classify the type of improvement, for example redecoration work, building repair or maintenance, a management or policy change or the provision of auxiliary aids and services. Categories may attribute recommendations to particular people or departments in an organisation, for example highways, estates, maintenance, human resources, information technology and so on. Categories often reflect the structure of the client organisation and their mechanism for implementing recommendations.

Cost banding

Some clients require information on the cost of implementing the recommendations included in an audit report. This is understandable given that a consideration of the cost of an adjustment is likely to have a bearing on any decisions taken on how and when to proceed.

If an auditor has the necessary skills and experience to accurately assess the cost of improvements, there is no reason why cost

Cost bands

Example 1

Ref.	Cost band	Example of works
1	up to £1,000	Modifications to an accessible WC, supplementary signage
2	up to £10,000	New accessible WC, modifications to steps and approaches
3	£10,000+	Construction of an external ramp or replacing external stairs
4	£20,000+	Installation of new lift/lift shaft

Example 2

Cost band	Value of works
A	£0–£500
B	£500–£1,000
C	£1,000–£5,000
D	£5,000–£10,000
E	above £10,000

estimates should not be incorporated into the audit report. The relevant skills are likely to be demonstrated by qualifications in building or quantity surveying, architecture or building management, but current experience is also relevant in order to take account of regional cost variations and other fluctuations in the construction market.

Cost estimates provided within an audit report are likely to be based on an initial inspection of the building only. It is unlikely that detailed investigations will have been made concerning the building fabric or any form of consultation held with a structural engineer. For this reason, any cost advice included in the audit report will be subject to verification following further investigations and should be clearly set out as such.

Given the limitations of providing accurate cost advice at the initial audit stage, it may be preferable to consider the use of cost bands which provide a useful indication of the likely magnitude of cost for each recommendation. Cost bands can be tailored to suit the range

and type of work likely to be required for a particular site or building, and can be as narrow or as broad as a client and auditor consider appropriate.

The provision of cost information in any form can be an effective way of highlighting improvements which can be achieved at no cost. Recommendations in a report should include improvements or changes to, for example, policies, staff attitudes, building management procedures and the method of service delivery, many of which could be implemented with no financial outlay.

The cost band information provides an indication of the estimated cost of each recommendation. This information is provided to assist the client prepare budget estimates and future expenditure profiles for implementation of the works. The cost bands represent the net cost of the works and should be regarded as a ball park figure only at this stage. The figures do not include VAT, statutory approval fees or consultant fees.

Case studies

The following three case studies illustrate the role of access auditing in planning and carrying out improvements to premises and services.

Case study 1 – Janet Maitland Hair Excellence

Service provider:	Janet Maitland Hair Excellence
Business type:	Health and beauty salon and training academy
Location:	Durham
Access audit:	Undertaken in house by owner of business to identify ways of improving salon services to provide for full access by all potential customers

Janet Maitland Hair Excellence, a leading health, beauty and hairdressing salon in the north east, achieved an award in the 2004 *Access all Areas* Awards for 'innovation and commitment to improving access for disabled people'.

The salon, defined as a service provider under Part 3 of the Disability Discrimination Act 1995, was recognised for its exceptional commitment to equality of opportunity, dedicated customer service and an enlightened approach to business investment, which has resulted in a highly successful salon and training establishment, with a deserved reputation throughout the north east and an expanding customer base.

A dedication to the delivery of the best possible service to all customers extends across all aspects of the business but is most apparent in the interaction between staff, trainees and customers and in the inherent accessibility of the modern salon.

Physical adjustments

The ground floor of the building comprises a salon, basin area, office/staff room and the academy space. The salon itself, however, has not always been as physically accessible as the owners, Janet Maitland and Peter McDermott, would have preferred, but a commitment to investment in the business provided the opportunity for a substantial refurbishment, which was completed in May 2003.

Prior to the refurbishment, Peter McDermott, a director and co-owner of the business, undertook an access audit of the existing salon and identified a number of areas which could be improved. These included:

- a single step at the door threshold and a change in level between the two adjacent properties
- a high reception desk which was positioned immediately opposite the door and left minimal space for circulation
- a waiting area with a low, soft sofa, no alternative seating styles and no space for wheelchair users
- restricted circulation space within the styling area due to the position of a central pillar
- restricted space in the washbasin area

Peter prepared a brief for architect John Hitchman of Hedley and Hitchman in Durham.

The brief was threefold:

- to create as much space as possible
- to include ramps to bridge the changes in level between the two adjacent properties
- to provide access for wheelchair users throughout the ground floor, including both the salon and training academy

The resulting refurbishment is very open and welcoming, accessible throughout to all customers and equipped with the latest salon accessories and facilities. The salon staff are pleased with the refurbishment too and have all found it a far more pleasant environment in which to work.

The single step at the entrance has been eliminated by reducing the internal floor level immediately inside the door and providing a shallow ramp up to the new reception area. The entrance door is wide, has a level threshold and a clear glazed panel to promote good visibility into and out of the salon.

The reception desk has been repositioned and is now directly opposite the top of the ramp where it is clearly visible and approachable by all clients. The hi-tech design of the desk complements the overall salon aesthetic. The low, soft sofa in the waiting area has been replaced with individual seats which are suitable for a wider range of customers but can also be easily removed or relocated if additional space is required for wheelchair users or baby buggies.

The styling area has been transformed. The area is light, open and remarkably spacious, with ample space for circulation even on busy days. This has been achieved in part by removing the central pillar (which was non-structural) and relocating the washbasins to the rear 'relaxation' room. Each of the ten new styling positions, which are now all located on two sides of the styling area, comprise a wall-mounted mirror, shelf and an adjustable-height seat. A range of styling seats are available to suit different customer

needs and the seat can also be removed if a wheelchair user prefers to remain seated in their wheelchair.

The salon washbasins are now located in a separate room to the rear of the styling area which is promoted as the 'relaxation room'. The fixed-height washbasins each have a luxurious fully-adjustable reclining chair with an integral (but optional) back massager. Staff noted that customers often opt for a relaxation session and head massage without a styling appointment, which is testimony to the ambience and comfort of this new facility. For customers for whom the reclining seats and fixed washbasins are unsuitable, a free-standing adjustable-height basin is available. This is fully portable and has proved a very effective and low-cost alternative means of ensuring the full range of services are available in the salon to all customers.

Training academy

The training academy, based primarily in the adjacent premises, comprises a large training room and staff room shared with the salon staff. All the doors in the salon, staff and training areas have a clear width of 870mm and large pull-handles. Circulation routes are kept clear, as are turning areas for wheelchair users.

Importantly, accessibility to the salon does not stop at getting in and around the premises. Two emergency exit doors are located at the rear of the building, one to the salon and one to the rear of the training academy. Both doors have a level threshold and lead through the rear yard to a passage along the side of the salon and back to the main street.

Staff training

Aside from Janet and Peter's commitment to customer service, the other side of their

Before May 2003, a central pillar restricted access and circulation on the salon floor

business – the hairdressing academy – has also benefited from their inclusive approach. The schooling that students and trainees receive includes equal opportunities, health and safety and NVQ reception skills. The importance of lip-reading is also stressed and staff are instructed to communicate with clients face to face, when cutting hair, instead of through the mirror.

A little bit of common sense, creativity and investment can go a long way, no matter what the size of the organisation. Janet Maitland Hair Excellence ably demonstrates how a small business, committed to customer service, can improve access to their service. They understand that access is an ongoing process, and that both management and staff must be responsive to customer needs and willing to effect changes if necessary. One member of staff commented that Janet Maitland Hair Excellence provides not only a good training experience but also a good life

experience. This is evident in their low staff turnover. Justifiably, the salon has received plenty of positive feedback from its clientele and is a deserved winner of an *Access All Areas Award*.

Movable chairs in the redesigned reception area increase flexibility of use

Case study 2 – Towneley Hall Art Gallery and Museum

Service provider:	Burnley Borough Council
Business type:	Local authority art gallery and museum service
Location:	Towneley Park, Burnley, Lancashire
Access audit:	Undertaken by Brian Towers, independent access consultant, prior to implementation of refurbishment project

Towneley Hall, Burnley, was the home of the Towneley family from the mid 13th century until the property was sold to the Burnley Corporation in 1902 for use as an art gallery and museum. The appearance of the Hall today is largely due to the work of architect Jeffry Wyatt, who added to the property during the early 19th century.

Towneley Hall itself is of significant architectural importance and is Grade 1 listed. The Hall houses an art gallery and museum with a variety of displays including natural history, Egyptology, local history, textiles, decorative art and regional furniture. The ground floor Regency Rooms are licensed for wedding ceremonies and the facilities in the new extension, including lecture and meeting rooms, can be hired for corporate events and educational activities.

Burnley Borough Council is defined as a service provider under Part 3 of the Disability Discrimination Act 1995 (DDA) in relation to the provision of goods, facilities and services at Towneley Hall. In addition, the Council is a major employer and is subject to duties under Part 2 of the DDA.

Towneley Hall underwent a major programme of redevelopment which was completed in 2002 and substantially funded by a Heritage Lottery grant. The project aim was to improve visitor access, enjoyment and understanding of a historic house, its surroundings and collections by improving interpretation and facilities. This was achieved by:

- building a new wing on the site of a servants' wing demolished in 1929 and relocating staff offices, the shop and sanitary facilities into the wing to release space in the old Hall for additional displays and period rooms
- providing additional facilities in the new wing, including an education room and library
- providing new displays in the existing Hall, updating displays and renovating existing period rooms
- changing the visitor flow around the building and improving physical access for disabled people through the provision of new ramps and lifts
- providing new forms of interpretation including audio guides, audiovisual presentations and computerised access to part of the collection

Access audit

An access audit was undertaken in 1998 by independent access consultant Brian Towers for architects Hurd Rolland Partnership. The access audit included a survey of the existing building and a review of drawings prepared by Burnley Borough Council illustrating the design of a proposed new wing.

The format adopted for the access audit report was a narrative format which enabled the auditor to describe in detail the existing features of the building and to highlight potential barriers to access. The report was structured into sections to follow a logical route through the building, starting with the entrance and the main public facilities, and followed by sections covering horizontal and vertical circulation, emergency evacuation, sanitary facilities, communication systems, lighting, signage. The audit included a record of the existing arrangements, features and potential barriers to access. Following this was an explanation of how improvements could be made, setting out options where appropriate.

Physical alterations

The access audit included a number of recommendations for improving physical access to the existing building, including:

- the provision of a ramped corridor and link to bridge the change in floor levels between a series of rooms at ground-floor level
- raising the level of the floor in one room in order to provide level access throughout the ground-floor galleries
- installation of a platform lift to provide an alternative means of access between the new entrance in the extension and the Great Hall
- the installation of a lift to serve all floor levels in the north wing
- the installation of a lift to serve the second-floor Long Gallery in the south wing

The most discreet physical modification to have been made to the Hall is the re-laying of the stone flags to a corridor to provide a shallow ramped route which links a series of rooms in the north wing, each of which was previously only accessible via steps. The re-use of existing materials and modulation of the corridor levels to match the existing floor levels within each room cleverly disguise the alterations, which are likely to be perceived by

Existing stone flags to the corridor have been re-laid to a shallow gradient and provide level access to a series of display rooms

building users as an original feature of the building.

Three further rooms, which were each previously linked by short flights of steps, have also been cleverly modified with the only evidence of change being a short ramp within the depth of an existing wall opening. The floor of the central room has been raised to match the level of the two adjoining areas and thereby provides level access throughout. Again, the adaptations have been sensitively implemented and, to the majority of building users, unlikely to be identifiable. The original floor boards were reinstated and an existing fireplace and hearth raised to match the new floor level. The original floor to ceiling height was sufficient to accommodate a reduction without compromising the overall proportions of the room.

A new ramp within a deep wall opening provides access to a suite of rooms previously only accessible via steps. The floor level of the room at the upper end of the ramp has been discreetly raised to match the floor level of two further adjoining rooms, thereby providing level access throughout

The existing change in level between the main hall and west wing necessitated the installation of a platform lift. The lift, while itself utilitarian in design, has been cleverly installed behind a new panel in the corner of the kitchen and accessed via a masonry wall opening to the upper-level passage. The lift provides a convenient alternative route immediately adjacent to a short flight of steps, and thereby enables continuity of journey sequence throughout the building for all visitors.

The area now occupied by the lift was previously a store and not immediately visible to visitors viewing the kitchen display. The lift is screened on one side by timber panelling, fabricated to match the original wall panelling to this side of the kitchen.

The platform lift sits neatly against a backdrop of original building features, including timber wall panelling and a corbelled stone arch

A new passenger lift was installed in the north wing and now provides access to all three storeys in this part of the building. Access to the Long Gallery at second-floor

The wall panelling was brought forward to conceal the platform lift enclosure and to retain the full display area inside the kitchen

level in the south wing is via a cantilevered stair to the south of the Great Hall. As the Great Hall (and ceiling void above) extends to the full height of the building, access is not possible for visitors between the upper floors of the north and south wings. A recommendation was therefore made in the access audit to install an additional passenger lift within an existing central passage between the two Regency Rooms at ground-floor level and two bedroom displays at second-floor level in the south wing to provide an alternative means of access to the Long Gallery. While this was a viable proposal in physical and operational terms, it proved to be too costly to undertake as part of the redevelopment programme and has not yet been implemented.

To ensure that visitors are able to experience the whole of the Hall, an orientation room has been established at ground-floor level and is accessed via the Great Hall. This room accommodates a large-scale model of the building and two interactive computers which enable visitors to take a virtual tour of the museum and its artefacts, including the Long Gallery. This is a good example of access to services and facilities being provided in an alternative manner where physical access has not yet been achieved for all building users.

Case study 3 – Greggs plc

Service provider:	Greggs and Bakers Oven
Business type:	Bakers
Location:	Nationwide
Access audit:	In house and by Configure Ltd

The commitment to developing a corporate access strategy and an ongoing programme of physical improvements to over 1,200 retail units, bakeries, manufacturing plants, distribution centres and offices, makes Greggs a good example of how a large retail organisation has responded proactively to its duties under the DDA.

Greggs plc is the country's largest independent bakery-related retailer, with high street outlets Greggs and Bakers Oven and a national workforce of over 17,500. The company has a strong commitment to its staff, shareholders and customers and, in line with its values, aims to treat everyone with dignity, equality and respect.

Greggs' stated aim is to 'work with its Divisions to eliminate barriers which prevent disabled people in any of its service centres, offices or retail units from making full use of goods, services and facilities'.

Access audits

As a starting point in the process of implementing change, Greggs established a steering group comprising representatives of the business's key disciplines, including managing directors, designers, property, health and safety, environment, production, sales and personnel. The steering group was responsible for identifying priorities, drawing up a strategy for implementation and drafting and adopting policies. Greggs has ensured that policies developed in response to the DDA are consistent and integrate with other corporate policies such as employment, service provision and health and safety.

With a property portfolio the size of Greggs, the process of auditing premises was a significant task. Initially, basic audits were carried out of each retail outlet to identify key issues such as door widths, steps, ramps, level changes and so on. Specialist disability advisory organisation, Configure, which advises and carries out access audits and staff training, was appointed to carry out additional audits for the more complex units such as the bakeries, factories and office premises, as well as the Bakers Oven outlets.

Access plan

Information gathered in the audits was recorded and formed the basis of an overall corporate Access Plan. Each property will eventually have an individual Access Plan which will identify specific improvements, set out a programme for the work and record progress made. The Access Plan is regarded as an evolving document and records the current position of each unit in terms of accessibility.

One of the key objectives of the Access Plans was to demonstrate how Greggs continues to recognise the need to provide accessible services to all of its customers and to provide employment opportunities in a non-discriminatory manner.

Horsefair, Bristol – steps have been removed to create level access

Staff training

In parallel with the process of identifying and implementing physical changes to premises, Greggs has established a programme of staff training on the DDA across the whole business. This training built upon the existing knowledge and awareness of staff which, it was found during the process of auditing premises, was in fact already comprehensive. To formalise and enhance this level of knowledge, Greggs introduced a programme of disability equality training to help shop staff, in particular, further understand and meet the needs of disabled customers. All new staff receive similar training as an integral part of their induction process. All shop design staff are currently receiving training and advice as to how to approach the design and procurement process.

Greggs has found that the key to ensuring a continued awareness of current legislation and disability issues throughout the business has been effective communication. The process of implementing change started with the establishment of the steering group, followed by comprehensive staff training, regular newsletters and Board statements. Greggs is confident in saying that the message has been filtered throughout the business.

The corporate and individual Access Plans have identified a programme of physical improvements which are currently being undertaken. Greggs has also introduced an access policy and has developed working relationships with specialist organisations that have provided expert guidance and advice.

Barrow in Furness – liaising with the local authority resulted in a raised pedestrian pathway affording access to the shop

Extract from an audit report

The following is an extract from the report of an audit of the Tunbridge Wells Museum and Art Gallery, Kent, and part of an access action plan based on the audit.

The extract is not a complete audit report and covers only a selection of items from the introduction and a selection of building elements – the approach and entrances.

The sample contents page lists items that would be included in a typical audit report.

Access audit report

Tunbridge Wells Museum and Art Gallery

Contents

Introduction

- Client brief/scope of audit
- Criteria for assessment
- Legislative context
- Disclaimer
- Explanation of prioritisation
- Management and other factors contributing to accessibility
- Means of escape considerations
- Audit details
- Glossary
- Description of building
- Consultation
- Summary of findings

Audit report

- Information and wayfinding
- Approaches
- Entrances

- Vertical circulation
- Horizontal circulation
- Galleries
- Collections Store
- Interpretation
- Staff areas
- WCs
- Emergency egress

Appendices

- General recommendations
- Plans as supplied

Introduction

Client brief and scope of works

This access audit report has been produced for the Tunbridge Wells Museum and Art Gallery (the Museum). The audit is part of a larger project being undertaken by the Gallery to develop an access plan and proposals to improve access to the building, services and facilities.

The audit is an assessment of the accessibility and usability of the staff and public areas of the building for disabled people. However, it should be noted that the issues considered in the report would affect the convenience of access to and use of the buildings for all its occupants, not just those with identifiable disabilities. The approach advocated is based on inclusive design principles, which aim to improve the usability of the building and services for all users regardless of age, ability or gender.

The audit report covers the approaches and the entrance to the building, circulation within the building and all public facilities and services. Orientation and wayfinding, information, display and interpretation are also covered.

The report records and assesses the current situation with regard to specific physical elements, management procedures, staff awareness and training, noting problems and giving recommendations to improve access and usability. Generally, only those items that fall below an acceptable standard are noted.

Criteria for assessment

The criteria for assessment are the:

- need to maximise access to and use of the building and facilities for members of the public and staff
- financial and practical considerations of access improvements
- provisions in *Approved Document Part M, Access to and use of buildings, 2004,* Building Regulations 2000, Office of the Deputy Prime Minister
- guidance in BS 8300:2001 *Design of buildings and their approaches to meet the needs of disabled people – Code of Practice,* British Standards Institution
- current guidance on the provisions of the Disability Discrimination Acts 1995 and 2005
- Code of Practice *Employment and Occupation,* Disability Rights Commission, 2004
- Code of Practice *Rights of Access to Goods, Facilities, Services and Premises,* Disability Rights Commission, 2002
- currently published good practice in design and detailing which meets the needs of disabled people, including:
  - *Easy Access to Historic Buildings,* English Heritage, 2004
  - *Inclusive Mobility: A Guide to Best Practice on Access to Pedestrian and Transport Infrastructure,* Department of Transport, 2002
  - *Designing for Accessibility,* CAE/RIBA Enterprises, 2004

- BS 5588:Part 8 *Fire precautions in the Design, Construction and Use of Buildings – Code of Practice for Means of Escape for Disabled People,* British Standards Institute (BSI), 1999
- *Personal Emergency Egress Plans,* The Northern Officers Group, 1993
- *A design guide for the use of colour and contrast to improve the built environment for visually impaired people,* Dulux Technical Group, ICI Paints, 1997
- *Colour Contrast and Perception, Project Rainbow,* Bright, Cook and Harris, 1997
- *Sign Design Guide – A guide to inclusive signage,* P Barker and J Fraser, Joint Mobility Unit and the Sign Design Society, 2004
- *Code for interior lighting,* Chartered Institution of Building Services Engineers (CIBSE), 1994
- *Specifiers' Handbooks for Inclusive Design: Platform Lifts,* CAE/RIBA Enterprises, 2005
- BS 5776:1996 *Specification for powered stairlifts,* BSI, 1996
- BS EN 81–70:2003 *Safety rules for construction and installation of lifts – Particular applications for passenger and goods passenger lifts,* BSI 2003
- *Disability Portfolio Resource*: The Council for Museums, Archives and Libraries, 2003

Dimensional criteria used in the report are based on the guidance given in Approved Document Part M, 2004, of The Building Regulations 2000 and BS 8300:2001.

Legislative context

The Disability Discrimination Act 1995 (DDA) places duties on employers (Part 2) and providers of goods, facilities and services (Part 3) not to unjustifiably discriminate against disabled people in the way they provide employment or services and for a reason that relates to a person's disability.

Extract from an audit report

Part 2 of the DDA places duties on all employers not to unjustifiably treat disabled people less favourably than others for a reason relating to their disability, and to make reasonable adjustments to assist disabled employees or applicants for employment. This may include changing the physical features of the premises if these put the disabled person at a substantial disadvantage compared to people who are not disabled. This is not a general or anticipatory duty but is triggered when a disabled person applies for a job, is employed or when an employee becomes disabled.

Part 3 of the DDA places duties on those providing goods, facilities and services to the public and makes it unlawful for them to discriminate against disabled people in certain circumstances. These duties are general, evolving and anticipatory.

While the DDA does not directly require accessible environments to be provided for disabled people, either in their place of work, or for access to goods, facilities and services, duties under the DDA include the requirement to make reasonable adjustments to remove physical barriers to access. Several factors have a bearing on whether an adjustment is reasonable: effectiveness, practicality, cost and disruption, and financial resources. The DDA does not require a service provider to adopt a particular way of meeting its obligations, and outlines options to remove, alter or provide a means to avoid the physical feature which may prove to be a barrier, or to provide a reasonable alternative method of making the service available to disabled people.

The Disability Rights Commission (DRC) has published Codes of Practice for DDA Parts 2 and 3, which provide further guidance.

The Museum has duties under Part 2 of the Act in relation to its employees and staff premises, and under Part 3 of the Act in relation to the services it provides to the general public and the premises from which it provides them.

The access audit is a useful first step towards meeting the requirements of the DDA. The findings of an audit can be used to prepare an access plan that will comprise a programme of implementation of improvements over a period of time.

The DDA does not include building design guidance, and it is advisable to follow current best practice design guidance, as provided by this report, to be able to justify decisions made.

The DDA does not override other legislation relating to buildings, such as planning permission, building regulations, listed building consent and fire regulations.

Disclaimer

This report has been prepared with reference to a view of current best practice which is subject to change. As the Disability Discrimination Act 1995 is not compliance based, adherence to the advice contained in this report cannot ensure compliance with the Disability Discrimination Act 1995 or immunity from the award of damages under the Act.

For information regarding any issues arising from the interpretation of the Disability Discrimination Act, it is strongly recommended that you seek appropriate legal advice.

Explanation of priorities

The recommendations are indicated as:

- short term, where considered immediate priority to meet DDA duties, and also to apply best practice, where easy to implement within current resources
- medium term, where adjustment may be appropriate as part of proposed refurbishment plans
- long term, where beyond the scope of refurbishment

Factors contributing to accessibility

There are many factors contributing to accessibility, the most obvious being the physical environment, including fixtures, fittings, furniture and equipment. It is also important to consider management policies and procedures which affect how a building will be used.

Appropriate awareness and attitudes of staff need to be developed if the safe and convenient use of the building and delivery of service is to be preserved. For these reasons, it is critical to consider staff training and management procedures as well as physical improvements to the building.

Means of escape considerations

Means of escape for disabled people, including the fire alarm system and management procedures for evacuation, were not reviewed as part of this audit. However, the following points should be noted.

A truly accessible building is one which people not only enter and use safely and conveniently, but which they can leave safely in the event of an emergency. Safe access is totally dependent on safe egress, and safe egress is of necessity planned egress. In general, two separate strategies are required for visitors and staff.

The individual needs of staff can be assessed in advance, agreed with them, and Personal Emergency Escape Plans (PEEPs) devised for all members of staff requiring assistance.

The needs of visitors are not necessarily known, and often their total knowledge of a building is the route by which they entered. As opposed to personal plans, an overall strategy is needed to allow visitors to escape from the building, or at least to a place of relative safety or refuge, whether assistance is needed or not. Specific measures to meet the needs of disabled people may include

alterations to an alarm system by introducing, for example, vibrating pagers, and by designating appropriate refuge areas.

This issue is discussed in more detail in a later section of the audit report.

Audit details

- Auditor(s)
- Meetings with Museum staff and others
- Date(s) of appraisal

The audit of the Tunbridge Wells Museum was conducted on a bright clear day.

- Drawings/information available:
  Museum map leaflets
  A4 outline Museum plans

Glossary of abbreviations

The following abbreviations are used throughout the report. The numbering in the main body of the report refers to paragraphs or diagrams in the guidance documents.

BS 8300 British Standard BS 8300:2001 *Design of buildings and their approaches to meet the needs of disabled people – Code of Practice*, British Standards Institution

AD M Approved Document Part M, *Access to and use of buildings*, 2004, The Building Regulations 2000, Office of the Deputy Prime Minister

ffl finished floor level

ecw effective clear width

stairlift wheelchair platform stairlift

The organisation and the building

The Tunbridge Wells Museum and Art Gallery is owned and managed by Tunbridge Wells Borough Council. It is within a Grade II listed 1930s brick building shared with the Town Hall and Council Library. Both staff areas and galleries are located on the first floor of the civic complex and the Museum shares two street-level entrances with the Library. The main entrance is to the side of the town hall complex, and a secondary one, providing wheelchair access via a wheelchair platform stairlift in the Library, is in Monsoon Way.

The museum cares for, displays and interprets local history, Tunbridge Ware, dolls and toys, archaeology, agricultural and domestic bygones, and also natural history. The Art Gallery shows frequently-changing exhibitions. There are also outreach and education services.

Consultation

The auditor facilitated a single day of consultation with the local access group shortly after the audit was conducted and before recommendations were made.

None of the access group members was a regular visitor to the Museum, because of physical and interpretive barriers. Many of the comments related to inadequate public transport access to the Museum. It was noted that accessible parking bays were not easy to locate and identify.

It was felt that improvements should be aimed at making the main stepped entrance more accessible. The local access officer informed the group that there were plans by the Council to raise the level of the pavement to provide level access via the main entrance.

Consultation with the local access group is ongoing on a six-monthly basis while recommendations are implemented.

Please note that the size of the type in the next section has been reduced to allow it to be accommodated in this book. Normally, text in an audit report should be at least 12 point, and made available in large print and alternative formats as required.

Audit report

Approach, parking and wayfinding

Area	The current situation	Recommendations for improving access
Approach routes	Tunbridge Wells Museum is close to the town centre and a short distance up a steep road (1:10 gradient) from the train station.	Consider liaison with local accessible bus schemes or tours to offer a special dropping-off service between the station and the Museum.
Signage	There is no directional signage for the Museum from the station, or from the town centre.	Good signage provides orientation, which is particularly important for people who are uncomfortable about asking, or unable to ask for directions. It can also prevent unnecessary journeys, important for people who have mobility impairments. Appropriate signage from main public transport nodes and from the town centre should be provided as part of a consistent wayfinding system. This should include an indication of the length and accessibility of each route. It should include advice to visitors on the nearest public transport route suitable for people who may find the hill difficult. It is important that wayfinding systems are clear, concise and consistent and include simple, clear signs, using colour and tactile elements, with links to visitor information materials, maps and the website. These should be provided in alternative formats. (See section on Wayfinding and Information.)

External steps on approach route

| Pedestrian approach

External steps on approach route | The civic building complex in which the Museum is located is on a busy junction. There are two external flights of stone steps up to the street directly in front of the town hall entrance from the lower street level. However, alternative ramped routes on either side, avoiding the steps, are not indicated, or obvious at this point. | Consider liaison with the local authority and neighbouring occupiers or responsible bodies to ensure that, where feasible, there is a well-signed and continuous route from lower to upper levels to meet guidance set out in AD M 1.1–1.13. |
| | The steps have a white painted strip at the nosing on the going of each step, but no markings on the riser. This could pose a problem to visually impaired people ascending the stairs.

There is no tactile warning to indicate the steps, which could prove a hazard for visually impaired people. | It is recommended the local authority is approached to investigate possible adjustments and the feasibility of further highlighting the nosings and installing tactile warning corduroy paving placed at the top of the external steps to follow guidance in AD M 1.27–1.32. It is important that the installation is done so as not to present a trip hazard. |

Handrail to external steps

Area	The current situation	Recommendations for improving access
Handrails to steps	A flat metal strip handrail to both sides of the steps is painted black against grey stone and is reasonably tonally contrasted for visually impaired people. However, the metal is cold to the touch and the handrails do not extend beyond the top or bottom step and are not continuous along the landing between the flights. This could prove a barrier for visually impaired people and ambulant disabled people who use the handrail for orientation. There are no additional handrails dividing the flights into sections not more than 1.8m wide.	Approach the local authority to investigate the feasibility of upgrading handrails and installing additional ones, to meet both dimensional provisions and the requirement that handrails not be cold to the touch. It is helpful to retain a contrast between the handrail and the stone wall. See BS 8300 9.1 p 47.
Planting at entrance	There are plants in planters on both sides of the stairs.	Olfactory features can be helpful for wayfinding for visually impaired people. If scented plants are used, these can be indicated in audio-described directions, or other wayfinding information.
Approach route signage	The civic complex is a distinctive building, which makes it easy to identify. However, a large sign at the main town hall entrance does not indicate the location or existence of any of the two entrances to the Museum.	Consider approaching the local authority for a non-reflective, matt sign to indicate the location of and entrances to the Museum at the town hall entrance.

Designated parking bays at main entrance

Area	The current situation	Recommendations for improving access
Approach by car and parking	There are two designated accessible parallel parking bays in front of the main entrance to the Museum, of the right width, but with no hatched access and safety zone, 1200mm wide, around the bays. This is on the other side of the carriageway of the street in front of the Museum and car occupants need to cross the carriageway to enter the Museum. There is a section of dropped kerb to the pavement at this entrance.

There is no vertical sign indicating the bays. | It is recommended that bays are marked out to follow guidance in AD M diagram 2, 1.18 p 21. Each bay at 2400mm width × 4800mm depth requires 1200mm hatched safety route to sides and rear. See also BS 8300 4, pp 5–11.

Consider negotiating with highways authorities to move the parking bays to the opposite side of the carriageway, adjacent to the Museum, so that car occupants do not need to cross the carriageway to get to the Museum. In the short term, ensure a safe route across the carriageway for car occupants.

As the road surface lettering could be obscured by snow or leaves, it is important to provide a vertical sign at the kerb indicating the bays. |

Entrances

Main entrance

Views of the main entrance

| Main entrance visibility | The main Museum entrance is set back within the side wall of the civic building complex.

A decorative stone frieze above the entrance and decorative white glazing frame are distinctive and well-contrasted to the brick façade. This suitably highlights the entrance to the Museum for visually impaired people. | A pronounced or projecting entrance such as a canopy would make it easier to identify the entrance, rather than one that is set back from the face of the building. A canopy would also provide shelter to those preparing to enter. However, as this is a listed building, such an addition is unlikely to be appropriate or reasonable. |

Extract from an audit report

Area	The current situation	Recommendations for improving access and usability
Signage	Two projecting, vertically-hanging fabric banners at high level indicate the Museum entrance with vertical text in upper case letters and an image.	For signage to be legible, a combination of upper and lower case letters is preferred (such as Museum) rather than all upper case; it is also good practice to use horizontal rather than vertically aligned lettering, or to repeat words horizontally. This makes it easier for visually impaired people, people with dyslexia, people with learning difficulties and others to read information. See *Sign Design Guide* p 54.
Signage	An 'A' board, with further information is placed on the pavement outside the Museum during opening hours	Ensure that temporary signs are placed consistently in the same location, so as not to confuse people who rely on familiar routes, and not create a hazard or restrict routes. Also consider repositioning signage to avoid information being on a slope.

Freize above main entrance

Area	The current situation	Recommendations for improving access and usability
Signage	A decorative stone band set into the façade, at a height of 6000–7000mm from the pavement, has carved upper case letters, which read 'LIBRARY AND MUSEUM', in white relief against a white background. This is not easy to read due to the height of the lettering and lack of tonal contrast with the background.	It is unlikely to be appropriate to change or increase the level of tonal contrast to the letters in the high-level band.

Notice board at main entrance

Area	The current situation	Recommendations for improving access and usability
Signage	A glazed notice board, set at a height of 1600mm from pavement level, is fixed to the brick face at the left of the entrance. It provides information about opening times.	It is recommended that the notice board be replaced with a matt, non-reflective prominent sign at 1400–1700mm from the pavement level. This should be fixed to the wall at the side of the entrance and provide clear information about the Museum.

Sign at main entrance

Area	The current situation	Recommendations for improving access and usability
Signage	A sign positioned at 2500mm above the pavement, to the wall at the side of the entrance, with white upper case text on blue, indicates access for wheelchair users via the secondary entrance. There is no other information about the route and no tactile elements to the sign	This sign is too high for wheelchair users and people of short stature to read comfortably. It is recommended that signs are positioned within a band of 1000–1700mm above pavement level. A combination of upper and lower case letters is recommended. The symbol for the arrow should follow guidance in the *Sign Design Guide*. Consider providing information with tactile markings. Information about the provision of a wheelchair platform stairlift to access the Museum, and available assistance, should be given at this point.

Steps to main entrance

Extract from an audit report

Area	The current situation	Recommendations for improving access and usability
Main entrance stepped access	There are two steps up to the entrance door. There are no handrails.	It is recommended that the client investigate the feasibility of options to provide level access at this entrance.
		One option would be to remove the steps and replace these with a ramp within the building. This option would necessitate installing an automatically opening entrance door and a set-back inner lobby door. However, this option may affect critical internal space requirements.
		A second option would involve raising the pavement level at the entrance to the level of the ground floor.
		It is strongly recommended that the option to raise the pavement to the level of the internal ground floor is further investigated. It is important to ensure that the gradient is preferably less than 1 in 20 on both approach directions, and that complementary steps are included if the gradient is greater than 1 in 20, with clearly identified nosings and handrails.
		It is important that routes for people passing by, rather than visiting the Museum, are not compromised.
		It is important to retain the dropped kerb to the pavement. This should be kept within reasonable distance of the entrance and not increase travel distance. See AD M 1.6–1.13 pp 19–20 and diagram 1.
		It is important to seek expert advice and statutory consents and permissions may be required.
	There are white markings at the stone nosings which provide good contrast for visually impaired people However, the nosings are chipped and damaged, and the height of the risers is uneven, which could present a trip hazard for ambulant disabled or visually impaired people.	In the short term and while permissions or alternatives are being sought, repair damage to the nosings of the steps and provide handrails of appropriate size and height, that are contrasting to the wall and wrap around the wall to start 300mm beyond the bottom step.

Lobby at main entrance

Area	The current situation	Recommendations for improving access and usability
Entrance lobby outer doors	A set of framed and fully-glazed double doors, painted white, in a white frame, are held open mechanically during opening hours. The doors provide an effective width (ecw) of 1500mm, with equal door leaves.	If level access is achieved, an effective opening width of 1000mm for each leaf is recommended to allow access for wheelchair users. See AD M table 2 p 29. However, due to the listed status, it will probably not be a reasonable adjustment to widen the entrance to accommodate two leaves of 1000mm or to alter the doors to a single leaf door. It is recommended that doors are either held back (on magnetic fire release closures if required), automatic or power assisted. See AD M 2.8–2.21 pp 28–31.
	There is no visual manifestation on the glass.	It is recommended that a visual manifestation be added to the door to a height of 150mm, at 850–1000mm and 1400–1600mm from ffl See AD M 2.22–2.24 p 31 and BS 8300 9.1.5.
Signage	There are a number of signs on the walls within the entrance lobby which provide information about the different aspects of the Museum.	It is recommended that location of information is rationalised to bring important information together as part of a consistent wayfinding system. This should include simple, clear signs using colour and tactile elements with links to maps and plans, print and recorded information.
Entrance lobby inner doors	The glazed inner lobby double doors are framed in dark wood, with horizontal glazing bars, providing good visual contrast, and D-style handles at 570–1250mm from ffl, which were easy to grip. The opening force at the time of auditing was an acceptable 20–26 Newtons. The overall ecw was 1500mm, with equal door leaves.	If level access is achieved, an effective opening width of 1000mm is preferred for each door leaf. See AD M table 2 p 29. However, this may not be feasible due to reasons for the outer doors cited above. It is recommended that doors are either held back (on magnetic fire release closures if required), automatic or power assisted. See AD M 2.8–2.21 pp 28–31.
Finishes	A small, loose, open-linked rubber mat is recessed into the lobby floor.	It is strongly recommended, in the short term, that loose mats are removed. In the medium term, if level entry is achieved, a solid-type (not coir) mat, flush with other finishes, to a depth of 1500mm from the doors, is recommended. See BS 8300 9.1.3
	Finishes are a cream-coloured terrazzo floor, black skirting and cream-coloured walls, which provide adequate contrast for visually impaired people.	Retain contrasts to finishes in future redecoration of main building elements.
Lighting	There is a significant drop in lighting level in the entrance area, which would make it difficult for visually impaired people to adjust to the new light levels.	It is recommended to introduce a transitory or gradual light level change. 100 lux is considered minimum for circulation areas, according to CIBSE.

Low-level signage at inner foyer

Extract from an audit report

Area	The current situation	Recommendations for improving access and usability
Inner foyer signage	Routes to the Library and Museum are indicated with notices on foyer walls at 100–800mm above ffl in upper case letters, which is too low for anyone to read comfortably. Decorative arrows are used, which are confusing and not clear to follow. A sign indicating the stairlift in the Library has upper case letters on a reflective laminated background, positioned at 1670mm above ffl. This would be too high for wheelchairs users to read comfortably.	It is recommended that signs are positioned within a band of 1000–1500mm from ffl. It is recommended that simple, non-decorative arrows are used, with a long tail, solid colour and without a shadow line. It is recommended, in the medium term, to develop a consistent wayfinding system, to include simple, clear signs using colour and tactile elements, with links to maps and plans, print and recorded information. See guidance in *Sign Design Guide*.
Foyer finishes	The flooring is grey loop carpet, with a black skirting and cream-coloured walls	These finishes provide adequate tonal contrast for visually impaired people, which should be maintained.

Seating en route to museum

Seating	There is insufficient seating on the route to Museum.	Consider additional seating, with backs and arms, within the Museum and Library foyer, and outside the internal entrance to the Museum, for use on arrival.

Main stairs to museum

Area	The current situation	Recommendations for improving access and usability
Main stairs to entrance	The Museum galleries on the first floor of the building, are accessed from the main entrance only by a staircase.	It is strongly recommended that lift access at the main entrance to all floors is investigated. (See section on wheelchair platform stairlift.)
Finishes	The stairs to the Museum level are concrete with a terrazzo finish and with dark-coloured risers, 150mm high, and cream-coloured goings of 270mm, with a dark stringer. The width between the handrails is 1340mm.	The existing differentiation in luminance between riser and going is helpful for visually impaired people. The width and pitch of the stairs and number of steps per flight are within an acceptable range.
	There are chrome handrails at a height of 770mm from the pitchline, to both sides, which is below the recommended height of 900mm to 1000mm. These do not extend 300mm beyond the top and bottom of the stairs and are also cold to touch. The width between the handrails is 1340mm.	Investigate the feasibility of upgrading handrails to meet both dimensional provisions and the requirement that handrails not be cold to the touch.
		Where feasible follow guidance in AD M 3.51, 3.54–3.55 and diagram 12. See also BS 8300 8.1 pp 39–42.
		Consider tactile warnings on handrails extended beyond the top and bottom step where safe.

Internal entrance to museum

Top landing	The landing at the top of the staircase has period-style finishes, with a grey terrazzo floor, a black/green border line and black skirting. These provide reasonable colour and tonal contrasts.	It is helpful to retain tonal contrasts between finishes for visually impaired people to more easily understand and negotiate the layout. See BS 8300 9.1 p 47.
Internal entrance	A sign indicating the Museum is located above the entrance door and there is another sign to the side of the door. Upper and lower case letters are used; however, the text size is too small for the height of the sign.	In the short term, it is recommended that an orientation sign be added which would incorporate or relocate the existing information. Consider a position opposite the point of arrival at the top of the stairs rather than the side wall and from 1000–1700mm above ffl.
	There is no sign providing an indication of layout of the Museum spaces, or a directory of galleries.	In the medium term, consider a welcome and orientation panel at the entrance point at 1000–1700mm from ffl, as part of a consistent wayfinding system, to include simple, clear signs using colour and tactile elements with links to maps and plans, print and recorded information. See guidance in *Sign Design Guide*.
Entrance circulation	A postcard rack limits the approach and circulation area at the entrance.	It is recommended to relocate the postcard rack to keep the circulation area clear. Also, manage the space at the entrance to avoid clutter.

Extract from an audit report

Area	The current situation	Recommendations for improving access and usability
Internal entrance doors	Inward-opening double, fully glazed doors to the Museum, are held open during opening hours. There is a ramp down into the Museum of 1:10, over a distance of less than 1000mm, immediately at the doors. This would be dangerous if doors were kept shut, as a level landing of 1200mm length is needed at the top of a ramp.	Ensure doors are held open at all times or automatically during opening hours, as the position and slope of the ramp would present a hazard. Investigate options to provide a level landing of 1200mm, clear of the double door swing, before ramping down to the level of the galleries. The slope of the ramp should not exceed 1:12 and preferably should be 1:20.

Secondary entrance

Secondary entrance in Monsoon Way

Parking	There is prearranged designated accessible parking near the secondary entrance in Monsoon Way, but this is not available for Museum visitors and is also across the carriageway from the Museum entrance.	It is recommended that designated accessible parking and dropping-off areas are made available to be as near as possible to the secondary entrance. This should be within 50 metres of the entrance and should provide safe travel.
Entrance and signage	A sign located at 1000mm from ffl at the side entrance door at the Library indicates the stairlift route to the Museum. This is upper case text only, in white lettering on a blue background, which provides good tonal contrast. The double door opens with only 580mm ecw for a single leaf. There is a call button at a height of 1000mm at the side of the entrance, which is black against a white background and is clearly visible.	A combination of upper and lower case letters is recommended. The sign should point out the availability of assistance. In the long term, see recommendations for level access at the main entrance. In the long term, investigate a one-and-a-half leaf door to achieve 800mm ecw and consult with the local fire officer in relation to emergency egress. See AD M 2.8 to 2.13 p 29. In the short term, consider a visible and audible response system at between 750–1200mm from ffl with well-contrasted, large tactile or Braille signage, and buttons.
	Library staff respond promptly to the side door call button and Museum staff then meet wheelchair users in the Library.	Visitors are escorted; therefore, in the short term, it is recommended that staff open both doors as standard procedure for wheelchair users to enter.
Lighting	The open light source causes glare.	In the short term, it is recommended to cover the light source to create a diffuse, even light without glare. It is important this does not reduce overall light levels and 100 lux is considered minimum for circulation areas. It is recommended to introduce a transitory or gradual light level change.
Lobby finishes	Finishes are continuous with the stair area. A rubber mat is recessed into the floor.	Consider replacing the mat with a flush, solid-type (not coir) one. In the long term, it may be appropriate to review use of this space with a view to installing a platform or passenger lift.

Wheelchair platform stairlift to escape stairs

Area	The current situation	Recommendations for improving access and usability
Wheelchair platform stairlift and escape stairs	A wheelchair platform stairlift to access the Museum is provided at the escape stairs located in the adjacent Library. This stairlift is undignified and unsuitable for many people who cannot transfer from their wheelchair.	It is recommended that passenger lift access to all levels is investigated. In relation to this, it is important to seek advice from a structural engineer and consider the impact of this option. See guidance in AD M 3.17 to 3.34 pp 39–40, or BS EN 81–70:2003. If it is not feasible to accommodate a lift shaft to all levels, then investigate the installation of an enclosed platform lift from the entrance lobby to the first-floor landing. See guidance in AD M 3.35 to 3.43 pp 39–40. It is important to ensure that the stepped access is maintained and that the proposed lift and the existing stairs start and finish at the same location. If lift access is achieved to upper floors, then emergency egress procedures need to be planned to include consideration for disabled people. This may include provision of refuge areas. In the short-to-mid term only, it is recommended that a reasonable adjustment would be the continuing use of the existing Library lift.
	The stairlift is staff operated and staff are trained to assist with its use.	Ensure that staff are trained in equality and access awareness and in the appropriate operation of the stairlift. Review current egress procedures with the stairlift facility. (Also refer to Means of Escape section of the report.)
	It restricts the effective width of the escape stairs and cannot itself be used in case of emergencies. The width between the stairlift and the opposite handrail is only 850mm and from rail to rail, it is 1020mm. The stairlift platform is approximately 700mm square, which restricts the width at the top of the stair to 630mm.	If vertical lift access is achieved, it is recommended that the removal of the stairlift is investigated with the local fire officer, to increase available stair width and improve the escape stairs to follow guidance in AD M 3.51, 3.54–3.55 and diagram 12, p 42. See also BS 8300 8.1.

Extract from an audit report

Views of escape stairs

Area	The current situation	Recommendations for improving access and usability
Colour contrast	Walls are yellow, which provides insufficient contrast with the brown handrail. The handrail is not continuous along the landings.	It is recommended that the handrail be made continuous to both sides and greater tonal contrast to the wall is achieved.
Nosings	Nosings are not highlighted and some step edges are damaged.	Repair edges of the steps and add nosing markings to goings and risers with luminance and colour contrast
Lighting	Bare bulbs on the stairs create glare and shadow under the stairs.	It is recommended that a minimum of 100 lux be maintained on main routes and stairs, but without glare, reflection or shadowing. It is recommended to add a diffuse cover to lights without reducing the overall level of lighting.
Door to landing	A white door in a white frame at the top of the escape stairs to the Museum has a vision panel at 795–1685mm from ffl. It has 770mm ecw and is wedged open.	The minimum zone of visibility for a vision panel is 500–1500mm. If feasible, lower the existing panel to this height. See guidance in AD M 3.7–3.10. Also ensure adequate tonal contrast between the door and the frame when next decorating.
	The door leads onto a corridor within the Museum, rather than the Museum entrance or reception.	It is preferable that all visitors arrive at the same point within the Museum.

The Access Action Plan

The following is an extract from the action plan created by the Museum on the basis of the audit report, with support from the access auditor.

Abbreviations

Audience Development Officer   ADO
Museum Support Officer   MSO
Museum Manager   MM
Library Manager   LM

Aim/Item	Outcome/objective	Date S = Short M = Medium L = Long	Action	Responsibility
Approaches Improve approach by public transport	Enable public transport users to access building	M	Identify local bus and transport schemes	ADO
		M	Liaise with local bus schemes	ADO
		M	Offer drop-off service if schemes exist	ADO
	Enable users to make choices about visiting Museum	S	Improve information about public transport access	MSO and ADO
		S	Produce access leaflet/web info/ alternative formats	MSO/ADO
	Enable more users to make visit by providing facility	L	Consider arrival seating	MM
		L	Liaise with Library as part of redevelopment	LM
		S	Improve Museum information about parking	ADO
Improve parking facilities	Enable more independent and car/scooter users to visit the building	S	Produce access leaflet/web info/other formats	MM/LM
		M	Improve designated parking to meet AD M	MM/LM
		M	Consult with Highways Department on immediate improvements – part of redevelopment brief	MM/LM
Improve signage and wayfinding to building	Enable all users to 'read' building and entrance better	L	Implement consistent wayfinding system for Museum and Library	MM
		L	Improve access signage	MM
	Enable all visitors to find Museum/Library better	S	Identify Museum/Library on street signage to building	MM
	Enable users to make choices about visiting the Museum	S	Consult with Council signage group	MM
		S	Clearly indicate entrance location	MM
		S	New Museum sign for entrance achieved (two months after audit)	MM
		S	Provide visitor information about entrances and wayfinding	MM
		S	Produce access leaflet/web info/ alternative formats	ADO/MSO

Appendices

Access audit checklists

The checklists on the following pages each cover one element of a building or its setting. The checklists broadly follow the order and correspond to the headings in the CAE/RIBAE design guide, *Designing for Accessibility*. This is an up-to-date and user-friendly good practice guide based on the 2004 Approved Document M and BS 8300:2001.

The checklists are also available in PDF format on the DVD which forms part of this book. The checklists can be printed or photocopied for use on site, so that the pack can be used to audit a complex building or to audit any number of buildings. Individual checklists can be reproduced several times to record multiple elements of a particular feature, where necessary. For example, several copies of checklist 17 *Internal steps* may be required in a building with multiple stairs, particularly if the stairs differ in configuration.

The checklists are intended as aide-memoires to help you carry out as thorough an audit as possible and as source material for writing up an access audit report and/or talking through key recommendations with a client. Completed checklists do not in themselves constitute an access audit report.

Access audit checklists

External environment

1   Car parking
2   Setting-down points
3   Routes
        gradient, width and signage
        surfaces, planting and lighting
4   Street furniture
5   External ramps
6   External steps
7   External handrails

Internal environment

8   Entrances
        approach and identification
        entry control systems
9   Entrance doors
        manually operated doors (non-powered)
        manually operated powered doors
        automatic door systems
10 Entrance lobbies
11 Entrance foyers
12 Circulation
        open-plan spaces
13 Corridors
14 Internal doors
        manually operated doors (non-powered)
        manually operated powered doors
        automatic door systems
15 Surfaces
16 Internal ramps
17 Internal steps
18 Internal handrails
19 Passenger lifts
        doors
        controls
        surfaces
        safety systems
20 Platform lifts
        doors and gates
        controls
        safety systems
21 Wheelchair platform stairlifts
22 WCs
        general provision
        separate-sex facilities
        WC provision for ambulant disabled people
        unisex accessible corner WC

Fixtures, fittings and services

Building management

Communications

Car parking

1.1 Is there designated parking provision for disabled car users?

1.2 Is the proportion of designated bays compared to standard bays sufficient?

1.3 Are the designated bays clearly signposted from car park entrance?

- identified as provision for disabled drivers or passengers only?

- close enough to the main building entrance?

1.4 In multi-storey car parks, are the designated bays at the same level as the principal entrance and exit level?

1.5 Are bays adequately sized?

1.6 Can car doors be fully opened to allow disabled drivers and passengers to transfer to a wheelchair parked alongside?

1.7 Is there sufficient space for tail loading?

1.8 Are the bays level, smooth, even and free from loose stones?

1.9 Are the routes from parking area to buildings accessible, with dropped kerbs and appropriate tactile warnings?

Car parking

1.10 Are routes adequately lit?

1.11 Are ticket machines and entry
controls accessible?

General observations:

Setting-down points

2.1 Is a setting-down point provided at a convenient point?

2.2 Clearly signed to and from the site entrance?

2.3 Located as close as possible to the principal entrance (or alternative accessible entrance)?

2.4 Sufficiently sized to enable transfer from side door and for tail loading?

2.5 Level access provided between the vehicular carriageway and footway?

General observations:

Routes

Gradient, width and signage

3.1 Are footpath routes from the edge of the site to the principal entrance (or alternative accessible entrance), or from the designated parking area to the entrance, or to other main routes on site, predominantly level?

3.2 Where gradients between 1:60 and 1:20 are unavoidable, are level landings provided at intervals?

3.3 Where gradients are greater than 1:20, are ramps provided? (See checklist 5 *External ramps*)

3.4 Do paths have a suitable cross-fall gradient?

3.5 Are routes sufficiently wide?

3.6 Are passing places provided?

3.7 Seating provided at intervals on long or inclined routes?

3.8 Signage and landmarks to aid orientation?

3.9 Are vehicle and pedestrian routes clearly distinguished?

General observations:

External environment

Surfaces, planting and lighting

3.10 Path surfaces suitable?

3.11 Sound qualities, textures and colours of surfaces used to highlight routes?

3.12 Joints between paving units suitable?

3.13 Edges clearly defined?

3.14 Drainage channels flush with path surface and designed to avoid trip hazards?

3.15 Planting used to identify routes or hazards?

3.16 Planting kept well trimmed?

3.17 Routes and hazards adequately lit?

3.18 Lighting well designed and positioned?

3.19 Guarding and cane-detection provided to low-level obstructions or hazards?

General observations:

Street furniture

4.1 Are pedestrian routes clearly defined and well planned?

4.2 Are routes defined using textural and tonal contrast?

4.3 Hazards and obstructions avoided?

4.4 Adequate headroom to pedestrian route?

4.5 Guarding and cane-detection provisions to areas with less than 2100mm headroom?

4.6 Bollards at least 1000mm high and visually contrasting with background?

- chains and ropes linking bollards avoided?

4.7 Items of street furniture visually contrasting with background?

- free-standing posts and columns highlighted using visually contrasting bands at the appropriate height?

4.8 Seating provided on long or inclined routes?

4.9 Cycle parking areas located clear of pedestrian routes and adequately highlighted?

General observations:

External ramps

5.1 Ramp accompanied by steps where the rise is greater than 300mm?

5.2 Ramp accompanied by an alternative means of access where the total rise is greater than 2m?

5.3 Ramp identifiable from approach route or clearly signed?

5.4 Ramp length and gradient suitable?

- wide enough to full length of ramp slope and landings?

5.5 Top and bottom landings of adequate size and clear of door swings?

- intermediate landings at regular intervals and of sufficient length?

- larger landings provided where it is not possible to see from one end of the ramp to another?

5.6 Maximum cross-fall gradient to ramp slope and landings?

5.7 Kerb upstand or solid balustrade to any open side of ramp or landing?

5.8 Surface suitable?

5.9 Slope surface visually contrasting with landings?

External ramps

5.10   Adequately lit?

See checklist 7 *External handrails*

General observations:

External steps

6

6.1 Steps identifiable from approach route or clearly signed?

6.2 Logical and consistent layout (avoiding curved flights and tapered treads and risers)?

6.3 Treads long enough and all of same length?

6.4 Risers shallow enough, all of same height, and unlikely to trip users?

6.5 Total rise of flight suitable?

6.6 Unobstructed width adequate?

6.7 Intermediate landings long enough and clear of door swings?

6.8 Step and landing surface suitable?

6.9 Hazard warning at top and bottom of steps?

- of correct style and detail?

6.10 Nosings effectively highlight step edges?

6.11 Lighting adequate and well positioned?

See checklist 7 *External handrails*

General observations:

External handrails

7

Repeat this checklist for ramps and steps

7.1 Are handrails provided in conjunction with a change in level?

- to both sides?
- of a suitable height?

7.3 Continuous along ramp slopes, stair flights and landings?

7.4 Extend beyond the top and bottom of the slope or flight?

7.5 Handrail profile easy to grip and suitable for providing forearm support?

7.6 Open ends of handrails designed to reduce the risk of clothing being caught?

7.7 Handrail surface suitable and not cold to the touch?

7.8 Visually contrasting with the background?

General observations:

Entrances

Approach and identification

8.1   Main entrance easy to find and clearly distinguishable from facade?

8.2   Alternative accessible entrance(s) clearly signed from the edge of the site and from the principal entrance?

8.3   Signage incorporates the international symbol for access?

8.4   All entrances clearly signed and visible from approach routes?

8.5   A level area provided immediately in front of all accessible entrances?

8.6   Structural supports clearly identified?

8.7   Weather protection provided?

8.8   Outward-opening doors adequately guarded?

General observations:

Entrances

Entry control systems

8.9 Door entry controls positioned in an accessible location?

8.10 Entry system usable by people with sensory impairments and by people who cannot speak?

8.11 Swipe-card system usable by people with sensory and mobility impairments?

8.12 Alternative gate access provided in conjunction with turnstiles?

General observations:

Entrance doors

9.1 Door opening wide enough for all users?

9.2 Adequate space available alongside leading edge for a wheelchair user to open the door while clear of door swing?

9.3 Level threshold?

9.4 Doors and/or frames visually contrasting with wall?

9.5 Doors and side panels incorporate vision panels?

- zone of visibility adequate?

9.6 Glazed doors: markings for safety and visibility?

- clearly differentiated from adjacent glazed screen?

- frameless glazed doors protected by guarding?

9.7 Door furniture: visually contrasting with door leaf?

- handles easy to grip and operate?

- within reach of all users?

General observations:

Entrance doors

Manually operated doors (non-powered)

9.8 Self-closing devices: door pressure kept to a minimum?

Manually operated powered doors

9.9 Door activation system (push pad, swipe card, proximity reader) positioned within reach of all users?

9.10 Clearly distinguishable from background?

Automatic door systems

9.11 Doors remain open long enough for slow-moving person to pass through?

9.12 Swing doors that open towards the user incorporate both visual and audible warnings?

9.13 Barriers positioned to protect access routes and guard against finger or body traps?

9.14 System incorporates a safety stop to prevent doors closing on a person passing through the doorway?

9.15 Doors revert to manual control or failsafe in the open position if power fails?

9.16 Revolving doors: supplemented by an adjacent accessible door in regular use?

General observations:

Entrance lobbies

10.1 Clear view in from outside to aid orientation?

10.2 Lobby large enough to allow a wheelchair user and companion to move clear of one door before negotiating the second?

10.3 Transitional lighting?

10.4 Inner lobby door meets same criteria as entrance door?

10.5 Weather mat of firm texture and flush with floor?

- of a suitable size?

General observations:

Entrance foyers

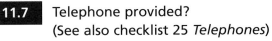

11.1 Clear view in from outside to aid orientation?

11.2 Routes from entrance doors/lobby logical, clearly defined and unobstructed?

11.3 Adequate circulation space?

11.4 Clear signage highlighting location of reception, WCs, stairs or lift?

11.5 Reception counter suitably positioned?
(See also checklist 24 *Counters and service desks*)

11.6 Waiting area: quiet and well lit?

- space for wheelchair users to sit alongside companions?

- range of seating styles to suit all users?
(See also checklist 21 *Seating*)

11.7 Telephone provided?
(See also checklist 25 *Telephones*)

General observations:

Circulation

Open-plan spaces

| **12.1** | Are circulation routes well defined? |

| **12.2** | Clear widths adequate? |

| **12.3** | Routes defined using contrasting floor finishes and textures? |

| **12.4** | Colour schemes maximise effective visual contrast? |

| **12.5** | Adequate lighting? |

General observations:

Corridors

13

13.1 Corridor widths adequate?

- unobstructed?

13.2 Turning space for wheelchair users?

13.3 Wall-mounted fixtures such as radiators and fire extinguishers recessed?

- if not recessed, items guarded with contrasting rail?

13.4 Any outward-opening doors in regular use recessed?

13.5 Where a series of similar doors along a corridor, doors consistent in opening width and direction of opening?

13.6 Corridor floors level?

- if not level, gradient as shallow as possible and incorporating regular landings?

- sloped surfaces clearly differentiated?

- gradients greater than 1:20 designed as an internal ramp? (See checklist 16 *Internal ramps*)

13.8 Internal lobbies: space for wheelchair users to clear one door before approaching second?

13.9 Natural and artificial lighting avoid
glare and silhouettes?

See checklist 15 *Surfaces*

General observations:

Internal doors

14.1 Is the door absolutely necessary for safety or functional reasons?

14.2 Effective clear width suitable?

14.3 Adequate space available alongside leading edge for a wheelchair user to open the door while clear of door swing?

14.4 Door distinguishable from surroundings?

- leading edge of non self-closing doors and doors which are held open, contrasts with door face and adjacent surfaces?

14.5 For double doors, the leaf in regular use clearly identified?

14.6 Doors and side panels incorporate vision panels?

- zone of visibility adequate?

14.7 Glazed doors: markings for safety and visibility?

14.8 Door furniture: visually contrasting with door leaf?

- handles easy to grip and operate?

- within reach of all users?

General observations:

Manually operated doors (non-powered)

14.9 Self-closing devices: door pressure kept to a minimum?

14.10 Electromagnetic hold-open devices or swing-free devices provided where appropriate and linked to the fire alarm?

Manually operated powered doors

14.11 Door activation system (push-pad, swipe card, proximity reader) positioned within reach of all users?

14.12 Clearly distinguishable from background?

14.13 Low-energy, powered swing doors capable of operating in manual, power-assisted and powered mode?

Automatic door systems

14.14 Doors remain open long enough for slow-moving person to pass through?

14.15 Swing doors that open towards the user incorporate both visual and audible warnings?

14.16 Barriers positioned to protect access routes and guard against finger or body traps?

14.17 System incorporates a safety stop to prevent doors closing on a person passing through the doorway?

Internal doors

Internal doors

14.18 Doors revert to manual control or
failsafe in the open position if power
fails?

General observations:

Surfaces

15.1	Floor surfaces suitable for passage of wheelchair users?
15.2	Junctions between floor surfaces correctly detailed?
15.3	Colours, tones and textures varied to help people distinguish between surfaces and fittings/fixtures and so on?
15.4	Floor surfaces slip resistant?
15.5	Cleaning regimes avoid making surfaces slippery?
15.6	Floor and wall surfaces free of confusing glare and reflection?
15.7	Textured surfaces to aid orientation for people with impaired sight?
15.8	Bright, boldly patterned floors avoided?
15.9	Busy or distracting wall coverings avoided?

General observations:

Internal ramps

16.1   Ramp accompanied by steps where the rise is greater than 300mm?

16.2   Ramp easily identifiable or clearly signed?

16.3   Ramp length and gradient suitable?

- wide enough to full length of ramp slope and landings?

16.4   Top and bottom landings of adequate size and clear of door swings?

- intermediate landings at regular intervals and of sufficient length?
- larger landings provided where it is not possible to see from one end of the ramp to another?

16.5   Kerb upstand or solid balustrade to any open side of ramp or landing?

16.6   Surface suitable?

16.7   Slope surface visually contrasting with landings?

See checklist 18 *Internal handrails*

General observations:

Internal steps

17.1 Steps easily identifiable or clearly signed?

17.2 Logical and consistent layout (avoiding curved flights and tapered treads and risers)?

17.3 Treads long enough and all of same length?

17.4 Risers shallow enough, all of same height, and unlikely to trip users?

17.5 Total rise of flight suitable?

17.6 Unobstructed width adequate?

17.7 Intermediate landings long enough and clear of door swings?

17.8 Step and landing surface suitable?

17.9 Nosings effectively highlight step edges?

17.10 Lighting adequate and well positioned?

See checklist 18 *Internal handrails*

General observations:

Internal handrails

Repeat this checklist for ramps and steps

18.1 Are handrails provided in conjunction with a change in level?

- to both sides?

- of a suitable height?

18.2 Continuous along ramp slopes, stair flights and landings?

18.3 Extend beyond the top and bottom of the slope or flight?

18.4 Handrail profile easy to grip and suitable for providing forearm support?

18.5 Open ends of handrails designed to reduce the risk of clothing being caught?

18.6 Handrail surface suitable?

18.7 Visually contrasting with the background?

General observations:

Internal handrails

Passenger lifts

19.1 Passenger lift available in a building of more than one storey?

19.2 Location of lift clearly defined by visual and tactile information?

19.3 Car dimensions sufficient to allow space for a wheelchair user and companion?

19.4 Clear landing space available at each floor level?

19.5 Landing level sign visible from lift car?

Doors

19.6 Lift door: opens wide enough for wheelchair users?

- visually contrasting with adjacent walls and floor?

- remains open for long enough to allow slow entry and exit?

- infrared or photo-eye door-safety override system installed?

Controls

19.7 Landing controls within reach of all users?

- distinguishable against background?

- visible from any position on the lift landing?

Passenger lifts

19.9 Lift car controls, including emergency call, located easily using visual or tactile information, and within reach of all users?

19.10 Audible indication of door movement, direction of travel and floor-level reached?

19.11 Floor level indicator visible and clear?

Surfaces

19.12 Lift car floor has similar frictional characteristics as landing?

19.13 Floor and wall surfaces suitable?

19.14 Areas of glass identified with markings for safety and visibility?

19.15 Half-height mirror on back wall of lift car to enable wheelchair users to reverse into and out of lift car and view lift landing?

Safety systems

19.16 Emergency call button within reach of all users?

19.17 Alarm buttons fitted with visual acknowledgement that alarm bell has sounded?

19.18 Emergency telephone/intercom available and easy to use?

  • fitted with inductive coupler?

General observations:

Platform lifts

20.1 Platform lift available as an alternative means of access to an adjacent stair or ramp?

20.2 Location clearly defined by visual and tactile information?

20.3 Designed and available for independent use?

20.4 Clear instructions for use?

20.5 Platform adequately guarded or enclosed?

20.6 Platform dimensions suitable for a wheelchair user and companion?

20.7 Clear landing space available at each floor level?

Doors and gates

20.8 Platform doors and gates: open wide enough for wheelchair users?

- visually contrasting with adjacent walls and floor?

- minimal door/gate opening pressure or powered door controls?

- door handles/controls within reach of all users?

Platform lifts

Controls

20.9 Landing controls within reach of all users?

- distinguishable against background?

20.10 Lift car controls, including emergency call, located easily using visual or tactile information, and within reach of all users?

20.11 Audible indication of platform movement, direction of travel and floor level reached?

20.12 Floor level indicator visible and clear?

20.13 Surface finishes and lighting suitable?

Safety systems

20.14 Emergency call button within reach of all users?

20.15 Alarm buttons fitted with visual acknowledgement that alarm bell has sounded?

20.16 Emergency telephone/intercom available and easy to use?

- fitted with inductive coupler?

General observations:

Wheelchair platform stairlifts

21.1 Wheelchair platform stairlift provided where a passenger lift or platform lift is unsuitable?

21.2 Location clearly identified?

21.3 Designed and available for independent use?

- or management supervision readily available?

21.4 Clear instructions for use?

21.5 Platform adequately guarded when in motion?

21.6 Platform dimensions suitable?

21.7 Platform neatly folded away when not in use?

21.8 Clear space at top and bottom landings for approach and exit?

21.9 Wheelchair platform stairlift does not compromise emergency exit route?

General observations:

WCs 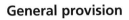 22

General provision

22.1 Is sanitary accommodation clearly identified?

22.2 In an accessible location?

Separate-sex facilities

22.3 Lobby of sufficient size for easy access?

- doors light enough to open easily?

22.4 Slip-resistant floors throughout?

22.5 Surfaces and fixtures provide effective visual contrast?

22.6 Cubicle door locks easy to operate?

22.7 Wash basins at suitable height?

- taps easy to operate?

22.8 Water temperature and heat emitters limited to a safe temperature?

22.9 In male WC, low-level urinal provided?

WC provision for ambulant disabled people

22.10 Is provision made in separate-sex facilities for ambulant disabled people?

WCs

22.11 Cubicle suitable size?

22.12 Door arrangement suitable?

22.13 Handrails provided to both sides of WC pan?

Unisex accessible corner WC

22.14 Is there adequate provision of unisex accessible WC facilities?

- in a suitable and clearly identified location?

22.15 Is travel distance to accessible WC facility acceptable?

22.16 If more than one accessible WC is provided, are the layouts handed (a left-sided approach and a right-sided approach)?

22.17 Compartment large enough to allow manoeuvring into position for frontal, lateral, angled and backward transfer?

22.18 Manoeuvring area free from obstruction?

22.19 Hand-washing and drying facilities within easy reach of someone seated on WC?

- taps easy to operate?

- temperature controlled?

22.20 Overall provision and position of sanitaryware and accessories suitable?

WCs

WCs

22.21 Sufficient space available outside toilet compartment for manoeuvre and door opening?

- door width adequate?

- door controls, lock and light switch easily reached and operated?

22.22 Assistance alarm provided, complete with cord, reset button and visual and audible alarm?

General observations:

Seating

23.1 Seats provided at intervals along long routes or where waiting is likely?

23.2 Seats stable, with armrests and provided in a range of heights?

23.3 Waiting areas:

- is there space for a wheelchair user to pull up alongside a seated companion?

- is there space for an assistance dog to rest?

23.4 Is there adequate visual contrast between seats and background surfaces?

General observations:

Seating

Counters and service desks 24

24.1 Counter height to suit seated and standing users?

24.2 Sufficient space to manoeuvre on both sides of the counter?

24.3 Provision on both sides for wheelchair users?

24.4 Sufficient space to write or sign documents on counter?

24.5 Counter surface and edges well detailed?

- effective visual contrast?

24.6 Adequate lighting to both sides of the counter?

- counter positioned to avoid silhouetting?

24.7 Induction loop and speech enhancement system provided?

- clearly signed?

General observations:

Telephones

25.1 Are telephones located where there is minimal background noise?

25.2 Is a telephone available at a height that allows easy use by wheelchair users?

- standing users?

- adjacent seat provided?

25.3 Clearly written instructions available?

25.4 Is there an integral inductive coupler?

- clearly signed?

25.5 Are textphone facilities available?

General observations:

Wayfinding, information and signs

Wayfinding and information

26.1 Overall layout of building reasonably clear and logical?

26.2 Audible public address systems supplemented by visual information?

26.3 Tactile maps or models provided?

26.4 Written guides and information well designed?

  ● supplemented with audio description and BSL-interpreted guides?

26.5 Specific textural systems of wayfinding explained at a central information point?

General observations:

Fixtures, fittings and services

Signs

26.6 Signs in a logical position?
- at an appropriate height?
- not obstructed?

26.7 Signs easily identifiable against their background?

26.8 Adequate visual contrast between text and signboard?
- signboard and background surfaces?

26.9 Suitable text style?

26.10 Symbols used to supplement text?

26.11 Consistent use of arrows?

26.12 Signs well lit?
- signboard surface minimises glare and reflection?

26.13 Tactile signs used where appropriate and positioned at a suitable height?

General observations:

Alarms, switches and controls

Alarms

27.1 Audible alarms supplemented by visual alarms?

- vibrating pagers?

27.2 Use of alarms an integral part of emergency evacuation strategy? (See also checklist 31 *Means of escape*)

Switches and controls

27.3 Switches, controls and sockets suitably positioned?

- designed for ease of use?

27.5 Effective colour and tonal contrast with background surface?

27.6 Clear indication of 'on' and 'off' position?

27.7 Appropriate use of tactile buttons and controls?

General observations:

Lighting

28.1   Lighting designed to meet a wide range of users' needs?

28.2   Level of lighting sufficient for intended use?

- PIR-activated booster lighting available?

28.3   Can building users control and adjust artificial lighting?

- natural lighting?

28.4   Stairs, other changes in level and potential hazards well lit?

28.5   Lights positioned where they do not cause glare, reflection, confusing shadows or pools of light and dark?

28.6   Fluorescent lighting installed only where it is unlikely to cause inconvenience to people with hearing impairments?

- artificial lighting compatible with other electronic and radio frequency installations?

28.7   Lighting does not undermine effectiveness of visual contrast in colour schemes?

General observations:

Acoustics

29.1   Acoustic environment suitable for intended use?

29.2   Background noise levels kept to a minimum?

29.3   Areas where communication is important located away from sources of noise?

29.4   Quiet and noisy areas separated by a buffer zone?

29.5   Good balance of hard and soft surfaces?

29.6   Environment free of unnecessarily obtrusive noise (for example from heating and air-conditioning units)?

29.7   Main power supply cables routed away from public spaces to avoid interference to hearing aid users?

29.8   Potential from interference by electronic equipment on hearing aids minimised?

Hearing enhancement systems

29.9   Hearing enhancement system provided?

- system suitable for location and intended use?

Fixtures, fittings and services

29.10 Wherever induction loops are fitted, risk of overlap minimised?

29.11 Where headsets, transmitter or receiver units are required (for example for infrared or FM radio systems) is the equipment readily available?

- in sufficient numbers for likely demand?

29.12 Appropriate internationally recognised symbol used to indicate the type of equipment available?

- signage clearly displayed?

General observations:

Building management

Are the following issues addressed by building management and checked on a regular basis:

External areas

30.1 Car parking: designated spaces not used by non-disabled drivers?

- kept clear of obstructions?

30.2 Bicycles stored clear of access routes and not chained to handrails of steps or ramps?

30.3 External routes, including steps and ramps, kept clean, unobstructed and free of surface water, algae growth, snow and ice?

30.4 Vegetation and planting kept trimmed to avoid:

- overhanging access routes?

- obscuring signage and the spread of light?

Doors

30.5 Door closers and door ironmongery maintained?

- side-hung doors accompanying revolving doors kept unlocked?

Circulation

30.6 Horizontal circulation: space required for wheelchair manoeuvre not obstructed by furniture, deliveries, storage and so on?

Building management

30.7 Vertical circulation: lifts, platform lifts and wheelchair platform stairlifts checked regularly for proper functioning?

WCs

30.8 Not used as unofficial storage areas?

- kept well stocked with toilet tissue, hand towels and soap?

- kept clean?

- waste bin not positioned in transfer area?

- transfer space not used as a storage area?

- assistance alarm cord hanging free and available for use?

Signage

30.9 New signs integrate with existing signage system?

- signs replaced correctly when removed for redecoration?

- temporary signs removed when no longer required?

- maps and models updated when necessary?

Hearing enhancement systems

30.10 Regular checks made to ensure equipment fully operational and effective?

- staff trained in using the equipment?

Building management

Alarms and security

30.11 Regular checks made of emergency evacuation alarm?

- WC assistance alarm?

- staff fully trained in response procedures?

Surfaces

30.12 Cleaning and polishing does not render slip-resistant surfaces slippery?

- junctions between different flooring materials do not become worn, presenting a tripping hazard?

- flooring when renewed is replaced like for like?

- redecoration does not compromise a carefully devised colour scheme?

Lighting

30.13 Windows, lamps and blinds kept clean to maximise available light?

- blown lamps swiftly replaced?

Information

30.14 Information readily available on the accessibility of the building?

- equipment available?

- assistance available?

- nearest accessible car parking and accessible WCs, if applicable?

Policy

30.15 Building management procedures and policies regularly reviewed and updated?

30.16 Is there an access action plan to carry forward information and recommendations from this access audit?

Means of escape

30.17 Exit routes checked regularly for freedom from obstacles (including locked doors) and combustible materials?

30.18 Alarm systems, including those in WCs, regularly checked?

30.19 New staff trained in alarm response procedures?

30.20 Overall escape strategy for visitors who may need assistance?

30.21 Personal emergency egress plan (PEEP) available for each member of staff needing assistance?

30.22 Both general escape strategy and personal emergency egress plans checked regularly for efficiency and effectiveness?

General observations:

Means of escape

31.1 Ground-floor exit routes as accessible to all, including wheelchair users, as entrance routes?

31.2 Vertical escape from upper or lower floors possible using a fire-protected lift with an independent power supply?

31.3 If disabled people cannot completely evacuate the building, can they reach places of safety or refuges?

31.4 Audible alarm system supplemented by visual system?

- vibrating pagers?
- mattress pads or pillows in bedroom accommodation?

See also checklist 30 *Building management*

General observations:

Information

32.1 Is information available in a range of formats, including:

- clear print?
- large print?
- Braille?
- telephone services?
- audio tape?
- digital (for example disk, CD ROM or file attachment)?

32.2 Is the information readily available?

Clear print

32.3 Does printed material follow clear print guidelines, including:

- a suitable font style and size?
- effective contrast between text and background?
- a suitable line length and spacing?
- a suitable word spacing and paragraph alignment?
- an avoidance of decorative text, text written at an angle or in curved lines?

32.4 Are the design and layout simple and uncluttered?

32.5 Are headings, photos, illustrations and text clearly differentiated?

32.6 Are photos and illustrations suitably sized?

Information

Large print

32.7 Do large print documents follow best practice guidelines, including:

- a suitable font style and size?

- effective contrast between text and background?

32.8 Can documents be readily produced in a font size to meet individual customer need?

32.9 Are large print documents as close as possible in format to the standard print version?

Braille

32.10 Is Braille information professionally produced to RNIB guidelines?

32.11 If any information which is not available in Braille, such as a complex and frequently updated catalogue, is an alternative available, for example a telephone information service?

Telephone services

32.12 Are contact telephone and textphone numbers clearly advertised and staffed?

32.13 Are textphone operators trained in the use of the equipment?

32.14 Are telephone operators familiar with the BT TextDirect service?

Communications

Audio tape

32.15 Do audio tapes follow best practice guidelines, including:

- speaker's voice clearly audible?

- structure and location of information clearly communicated?

- effective indexing of sections to enable easy navigation of tape?

Digital

32.16 Can information be readily transmitted on disk, CD ROM or via the internet (using email or downloaded from a website)?

32.17 Is the document designed in a clear, simple manner?

32.18 Is the information available (or able to be saved) as a text-only file?

32.19 Can digital information be tailored to suit individual customer requirements, for example by saving information as a particular file type?

See also checklist 33 *Websites*

General observations:

Websites

33.1 Has the website been designed in accordance with best practice guidelines, including:

- is the website logically structured and easy to navigate?

- is language simple and clear?

- is there effective tonal contrast between text, graphics and background?

- is there a text alternative to audio and image files?

- are unnecessary moving graphics avoided?

- are video sequences captioned, or is a link provided to a transcript of the audio and video content?

33.2 Does the design of the website offer the flexibility for individual users to adjust text and colour settings using their own browser?

33.3 Is the web designer familiar with international guidelines on web accessibility?

General observations:

Communication services

34.1 Are staff aware of or given training in the diversity of communication needs?

34.2 Are any staff trained and/or qualified to provide communication services?

34.3 Is there a procedure for arranging communication services, when required, including:

- British Sign Language (BSL)/English interpreters?

- communication support workers?

- deafblind interpreters and communicator guides?

- lipspeakers?

- notetakers?

- electronic notetakers?

- speech-to-text reporters?

34.4 Are communication services offered as an integral part of a programme of events, for example signed, audio described and captioned performances in a theatre?

General observations:

Sources of useful information

Organisations

British Standards Institution (BSI)
389 Chiswick High Road
London W4 4AL
Tel: 020 8996 9000
Fax: 020 8996 7001
Email: cservices@bsi-global.com
Website: www.bsi.org.uk

Publishes British Standards including
BS 8300:2001 (incorporating Amendment No 1)
*Design of buildings and their approaches to
meet the needs of disabled people – Code of
practice.*

Centre for Accessible Environments
70 South Lambeth Road
London SW8 1RL
Tel/textphone: 020 7840 0125
Fax: 020 7840 5811
Email: info@cae.org.uk
Website: www.cae.org.uk

Provides technical information, training and
consultancy on making buildings accessible to
all users.

Department of Finance and Personnel
Building Regulations Unit
Third Floor, Lancashire House
3 Linenhall Street
Belfast BT2 8AA
Tel: 028 90542923
Email: DFP.enquiries@dfpni.gov.uk
Website: www2.dfpni.gov.uk

For information on the Northern Ireland
Technical Booklets.

Department for Work and Pensions
Disability Unit
Level 6
Adelphi
1–11 John Adam Street
London WC2N 6HT
Tel: 020 7712 2171
Fax: 020 7712 2386
Website: www.dwp.gov.uk and
www.disability.gov.uk

Responsible for the Government's welfare
reform agenda, supports disabled people and
their carers, disability benefits and disability
civil rights issues.

Disability Rights Commission
DRC Helpline
Freepost MID 02164
Stratford-upon-Avon CV37 9BR
Tel: 08457 622 633
Textphone: 08457 622 644
Fax: 08457 778 878
Email: enquiry@drc-gb.org
Website: www.drc.org.uk

An independent body set up by the
government to prevent discrimination against
disabled people. Publishes codes of practice
and other guidance related to the DDA.

The Equality Commission for Northern Ireland
Equality House
7–9 Shaftesbury Square
Belfast BT2 7DP
Tel: 028 90 500600
Fax: 028 90 248687
Textphone: 028 90 500589
Email: information@equalityni.org

Works towards the elimination of
discrimination and keeps the relevant
legislation under review.

Sources of useful information

Employers' Forum on Disability
Nutmeg House
60 Gainsford Street
London SE1 2NY
Tel: 020 7403 3020
Textphone: 020 7403 0040
Fax: 020 7403 0404
Email: enquiries@employers-forum.co.uk
Website: www.employers-forum.co.uk

Represents and advises member companies
on disability issues, plus information on
good practice available free to all
businesses.

The Mobility and Inclusion Unit
Department for Transport
Zone 1/18, Great Minster House
76 Marsham Street
London SW1P 4DR
Tel: 020 7944 8300
Fax: 020 7944 6589
Email: miu@dft.gsi.gov.uk
Website: www.mobility-unit.dft.gov.uk

Research, information and policy advice.

National Register of Access Consultants
70 South Lambeth Road
London SW8 1RL
Tel: 020 7735 7845
Textphone: 020 7840 0125
Fax: 020 7840 5811
Email: info@nrac.org.uk
Website: www.nrac.org.uk

Enables clients quickly and easily to locate
suitable auditors or consultants, and provides
a quality standard for those advising on the
accessibility of the built environment for
disabled people.

Royal Institute of British Architects (RIBA)
66 Portland Place
London W1B 1AD
Public information line: 0906 302 0400
Tel: 020 7580 5533
Fax: 020 7255 1541
Email: info@inst.riba.org
Website: www.architecture.com

The RIBA advances architecture by
demonstrating benefit to society and
excellence in the profession.

Royal National Institute of the Blind (RNIB)
105 Judd Street
London W1H 9NE
Tel: 020 7388 1266
Fax: 020 7388 2034
Email: helpline@rnib.org.uk
Website: www.rnib.org.uk

Help, advice and support for people with
serious visual impairments.

Royal National Institute for Deaf People (RNID)
19–23 Featherstone Street
London EC1Y 8SL
National information line: 0808 808 0123
Tel: 020 7296 8199
Email: informationline@rnid.org.uk

Help, advice and support for people with
hearing impairments.

Scottish Building Standards Agency
Denholm House
Almondvale Business Park
Livingston EH54 6GA
Tel: 01506 600 400
Fax: 01506 600 401
Email: info@sbsa.gov.uk
Website: www.sbsa.gov.uk

For information on the Scottish Technical
Handbooks.

The Stationery Office Ltd
PO Box 29
Duke Street
Norwich NR3 1GN
Tel: 0870 600 5522
Fax: 0870 600 5533
Email: services@tso.co.uk
Online ordering:
www.tso.co.uk/bookshop

Sells printed versions of any item of legislation
or any other official publication previously
published by HMSO.

Publications

Legislation, standards and codes of practice

The Building Regulations 2000 Approved Document M: Access to and use of buildings (England and Wales)
Office of the Deputy Prime Minister
The Stationery Office, 2003

The Building Regulations (Northern Ireland) 2000 Technical booklet R: Access and facilities for disabled people
Great Britain Department of Finance and Personnel (Northern Ireland)
The Stationery Office, 2001

Non-Domestic Technical Handbook
Scottish Executive
The Stationery Office, 2005

BS 5588:Part 8:1988 Fire Precautions in the Design, Construction and Use of Buildings – Code of practice for means of escape for disabled people
The British Standards Institution, 1988

BS 8300:2001 (Incorporating Amendment No 1) Design of buildings and their approaches to meet the needs of disabled people – Code of practice
The British Standards Institution, June 2005

Disability Discrimination Act 1995
The Stationery Office, 1995

Disability Discrimination Act 2005
The Stationery Office, 2005

Code of Practice Rights of Access to Goods, Facilities, Services and Premises
Disability Rights Commission
The Stationery Office, 2002

Code of Practice for providers of Post-16 education and related services
Disability Rights Commission
The Stationery Office, 2002

Code of Practice for Schools
Disability Rights Commission
The Stationery Office, 2002

Code of Practice – Employment and Occupation
Disability Rights Commission
The Stationery Office, 2004

Code of Practice – Trade Organisations and Qualification Bodies
Disability Rights Commission
The Stationery Office, 2004

Other publications

Access Audits Price Guide 2002 for work in relation to the Disability Discrimination Act
Building Cost Information Service Ltd, The Royal Institution of Chartered Surveyors, 2002
Clear, concise, specialist guidance on the costs of alteration works and improvements that may be required to existing buildings.

Access for Disabled People
Sport England, 2002
Design guidance note including a series of checklists for auditing sports buildings.

Access to ATMs: UK design guidelines
by Robert Feeney
CAE, 2002
Design principles and guidance for those who design, manufacture, install and maintain ATMs.

Buildings for all to use 2: improving the accessibility of public buildings and environments
by K Bright, S Flanagan, J Embleton, L Selbekk and G Cook
CIRIA, 2004

Provides comprehensive advice on altering existing non-residential buildings to improve access for all building users.

Building Sight
by Peter Barker, Jon Barrick, Rod Wilson
HMSO in association with the Royal National Institute of the Blind
RNIB, 1995
A handbook of building and interior design solutions to include the needs of visually impaired people.

Code for Lighting
Chartered Institution of Building Services Engineers (CIBSE), 2000
Detailed guidance on all aspects of lighting.

Designing for Accessibility
CAE/RIBA Enterprises, 2004
Up-to-date and user-friendly good practice guide based on the 2004 Approved Document M and BS 8300:2001

A design guide for the use of colour and contrast to improve the built environment for visually impaired people
Dulux Technical Group, ICI Paints, 1997

Disabled Access to Facilities: a practical and comprehensive guide to a service provider's duties under Part III (2004) of the Disability Discrimination Act 1995
FM Law Series
by Ian Waterman and Janet A Bell,
Access Matters UK Ltd
Butterworths Tolley Lexis Nexis, 2002

Disability: Making Buildings Accessible – Special Report, Third Edition
Edited by Keith Bright
Workplace Law Network, 2005

Disability Portfolio
Resource: The Council for Museums, Archives and Libraries, 2003
Series of 12 guides on how to meet the needs of disabled people such as users and staff in museums, archives and libraries including

guides on the DDA, Audits and Accessible Environments.
www.resource.gov.uk/action/learnacc/ooaccess_03.asp

Easy Access to Historic Buildings
English Heritage, 2004
Guidance in relation to achieving access in historic buildings.

Good Loo Design Guide
CAE/RIBA Enterprises, 2004
Authoritative design guidance on WCs that meet the requirement of all users.

Guidance on the use of tactile paving surfaces
DTLR Mobility and Inclusion Unit, 1999

Inclusive Mobility: a guide to best practice on access to pedestrian and transport infrastructure
by Philip R Oxley, Cranfield Centre for Logistics and Transportation
Department for Transport Mobility and Inclusion Unit, 2002

Inclusive Projects: a guide to best practice on preparing and delivering project briefs to secure access
Disabled Persons Transport Advisory Committee, Department of Transport, 2003

Inclusive School Design – Accommodating pupils with special educational needs and disabilities in mainstream schools
Department for Education and Employment The Stationery Office, 2001

Planning and Access for Disabled People – A Good Practice Guide
Office of the Deputy Prime Minister, 2003
How to ensure that the town and country planning system in England successfully and consistently delivers inclusive environments as an integral part of the development process.

Sign Design Guide
by Peter Barker and June Fraser
JMU and the Sign Design Society, 2000
A guide to inclusive signage.

Specifiers' Handbooks for Inclusive Design: Architectural Ironmongery
CAE/RIBA Enterprises, 2005
Authoritative design guidance on architectural ironmongery that meets the requirements of all users.

Specifiers' Handbooks for Inclusive Design: Automatic Door Systems
CAE/RIBA Enterprises, 2005
Authoritative design guidance on automatic door systems that meet the requirements of all users.

Specifiers' Handbooks for Inclusive Design: Platform lifts
CAE/RIBA Enterprises, 2005
Authoritative design guidance on platform lifts that meet the requirements of all users.

Index